Track and Track Laying
IN RAILWAY MODELLING

Track and Track Laying
IN RAILWAY MODELLING

Brian Taylor

THE CROWOOD PRESS

First published in 2022 by
The Crowood Press Ltd
Ramsbury, Marlborough
Wiltshire SN8 2HR

enquiries@crowood.com

www.crowood.com

British Library Cataloguing-in-Publication Data

A catalogue record for this book is available from the British Library.

ISBN 978 1 78500 995 2

ACKNOWLEDGEMENTS

Many thanks must be given to Sandra Kitchener, who looked after me during the major operation I had during the time I wrote this book, and for her kindness. Thanks also to Charles Bendetto and Allen Etheridge of The Old Barn Model Craftsmen – compatriots in building many model railways. And to Kelvan Gale, for his encouragement; and to Karen of 'The Admin Tree', who typed up the manuscript for me.

Thanks are also due of course to all the suppliers who have supported me over the years, particularly J. Morris and Engine Shed/Gaugemaster.

Cover design by Maggie Mellett

Typeset by Shane O'Dwyer, Swindon, Wiltshire

Printed and bound in India by Replika Press Pvt Ltd

CONTENTS

INTRODUCTION

Many railway modellers were given model railways when they were children. I remember being presented with a basic Triang train set, which consisted of an oval of track and a 3F tank engine, with three wagons and a controller. I couldn't get near this for a while, since my uncle and my father spent Christmas Day playing with it themselves! Or so it seemed to me.

Doubtless psychologists would say that it was my initial frustration at not being able to get near my own first model railway that fuelled my later passion for all things to do with model trains, and possibly the real thing, too. My first memory of seeing a full-size train was actually of one running on the London Underground.

In 1960 the Bluebell Railway, which was really the first preserved standard-gauge line, opened just three miles from where I lived. In fact the true first was the Middleton Railway, but this was an industrial railway, not a familiar single track, country branch line.

The Bluebell's first engine was a Brighton Terrier – *Stepney*. I was used to seeing the Terriers, as they were a familiar sight at Newhaven Harbour, near where my grandparents lived. Terriers could be seen trundling along the A259 road and across the old swing bridge with a string of wagons, serving the wharfs on the West Quay. For many years a source of traffic was a tarpaulin works. Each wagon from the works had a label, showing

Station details. Sketches of line-side details drawn by the author on the Bluebell Railway, 1984.

TERRIER LOCOS

Seeing a Terrier on Newhaven Bridge was always a thrill. Towards the destination of the line, the train could be seen passing Newhaven's Napoleonic Fort, complete with moat and drawbridge. A little further down, the Terrier could be observed fussing around, shunting wagons in the fenced yard under the cliff. In the early 1920s a railway book described the Terriers as 'old veterans'. In 1922 some were fifty years old! Quite a few are preserved. Terriers are very popular models, of course.

its destination. Local children used to pay nocturnal visits and swop the labels over!

The West Quay line had gone by 1963, and so had the Terriers. Fairly quickly the contrast between what could be seen on the Bluebell Railway, and what were familiar sights on the rest of the railway network, became increasingly great.

In 1968 I went to college in Liverpool. When I paid a visit for an interview there, steam was still around in the area – but a few months later not a single steam loco was to be seen.

Of course, as things have turned out, there are now many preserved railways and plenty of steam engines running on them. Even without steam on the rest of the railway system, trains still fascinate young children, just as they have done since the days of Stephenson's *Rocket*.

In terms of modelling railways, this is still a very popular hobby, with considerable trade support. Branches of the hobby, which at one time seemed to

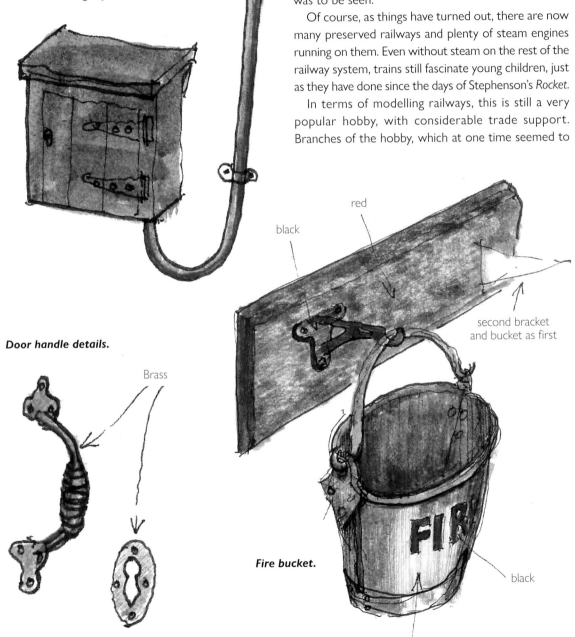

A box containing a phone.

Door handle details.

Brass

red

black

second bracket and bucket as first

Fire bucket.

FIR

black

red

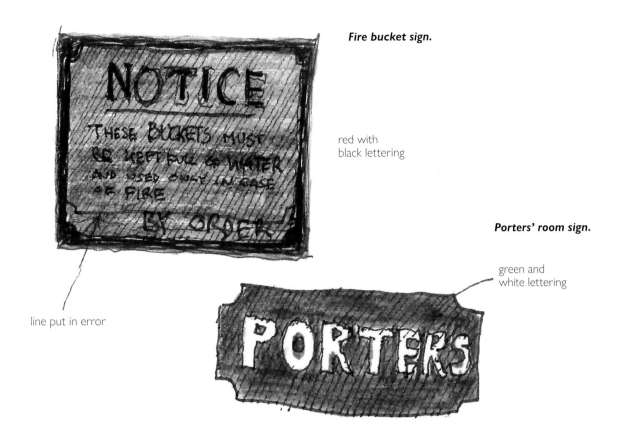

Fire bucket sign.

red with
black lettering

Porters' room sign.

green and
white lettering

line put in error

be quite obscure, such as narrow-gauge railway modelling, are now served by 'ready to run' items available across the counter or via the internet. This would have been unthinkable twenty years ago. Still, even with so many products available, for many people activities such as making baseboards, laying track and wiring up model railways seem frightening prospects. This book is about showing techniques and methods for building model railways from the ground up.

First, we will look at scales and gauges. Then, planning and designing layouts will be considered, and the pros and cons of different domestic locations will be examined. We look at baseboard construction for both portable and permanent layouts. After describing the construction of what is the foundation of a successful layout, we look at the track systems that are available – first, sectional track types, then flexible tracks, which can be successfully used together.

One of the objects of this book is to describe how to lay tracks and deal with the problems that can be

encountered along the way. We will also look at tools, and how to use and maintain them. For example, have you ever thought of servicing a hammer? We will also show how to develop the skills needed to make trackwork by hand, and even how to shape rails with a file.

There is no doubt that one of the greatest fears that potential modellers have concerning building layouts is wiring them up. We look at wiring in this book, and explain in simple language the various terms that go with it. How to wire up both analogue (DC) and digital layouts (DCC) is shown graphically. Finally, there are hints and tips on ballasting track, and also weathering.

As a preamble, the book contains a basic history of track, and takes a look at the various forces that influence prototype railways and determine the design of trackwork. Fortunately, when building model railways, we don't need to take too much account of passenger comfort and safety, both prime considerations on real railways!

CHAPTER ONE

A BASIC HISTORY OF TRACK

Guided forms of transport infrastructure are found across the world and have been around for a surprising length of time. The earliest known examples seem to have used grooves cut into stone to guide wheels. The first known example of this was the Diolkos wagonway, which transported boats across the Isthmus of Corinth. Wheeled vehicles ran in grooves cut into the limestone and were hauled by men and animals. The date was around 600BC.

By the 1700s, wagonways were in use across Britain, though there were far more in the north-east of England than elsewhere. Flanged metal 'plateways' took over from timber rails, but ultimately, flanged wheels ruled the day as they coped with curved sections of track more easily.

RAILS

By the time the famous Liverpool & Manchester Railway was opened, the need for stronger, heavier rails had been appreciated. These rails were T-section, and 'fish bellied' when viewed side on. A hangover from the very early days of railways is that the plates used to join rails together are known as fishplates. For many years, the men charged with laying the track were called platelayers.

Nowadays, most railway lines are laid with continuously welded rails. Previous to this, rails had been laid in 18m (60ft) lengths. Rails of this length were introduced by the London & North Western Railway in 1910, replacing shorter rails. The Great Western Railway originally used light 'bridge' rails on sleepers laid longitudinally. The track gauge was the very broad 7ft.

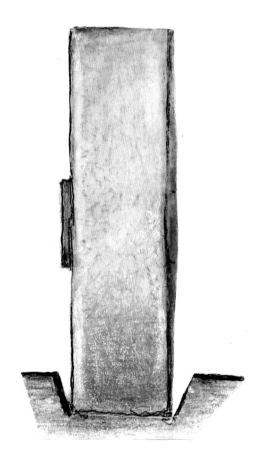

ABOVE: Wheel running in a stone groove.

RIGHT: Early rail.

Wooden chaldron waggon for carrying coal.

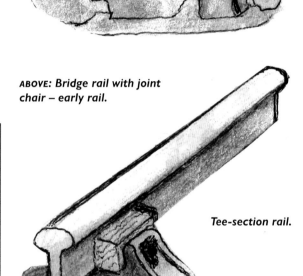

ABOVE: Bridge rail with joint chair – early rail.

Tee-section rail.

HITLER'S STRANGE RAILWAY

Many years after Brunel conceived his 7ft-gauge Great Western lines, Adolf Hitler envisaged an ultra broad-gauge railway across Europe. It seems that some planning was undertaken on this, as it was one of Hitler's pet projects. But unlike Brunel's broad-gauge lines, it never happened.

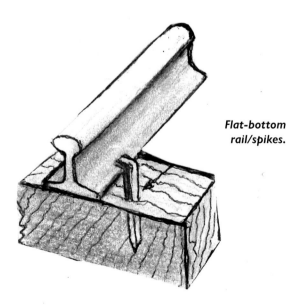

Flat-bottom rail/spikes.

Principally, two types of rail succeeded the earlier forms. The first, known as Vignoles rail, is now referred to as 'flat-bottom rail'. This type was invented by Charles Vignoles. With their cross sections like girders, they provided excellent support between the sleepers. Incidentally, the 'sleeper' name has been around since the seventeenth century, and denoted a beam sitting on the ground supporting the other beams. The American name for the same, in railway terms, is 'cross tie'.

Bullhead track dated back to 1863, and was invented by Joseph Locke. He thought that if a rail was the same section top and bottom, it could be inverted – when worn, it could just be turned the other way up. Unfortunately the bases received a pounding as well as the heads, so the idea proved impractical! Nevertheless, this type of rail section was popular. The

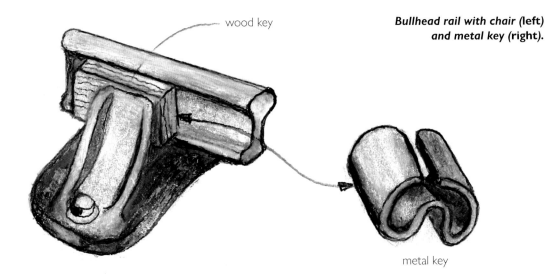

Bullhead rail with chair (left) and metal key (right).

rail head was increased in size for longer wear of the head. The base was supported by cast-iron chairs. The rails were held in place by wooden – later steel – keys, which were hammered into place.

It was common practice abroad to use dog spikes driven into rough-hewn timber sleepers to hold in place the flat-bottom rails, widely in use. This form of permanent way was rather looked down on in England, and was regarded as an inferior form of track.

The principal form of track in the UK for many years was bullhead with chairs, but the decision was made to change over to flat-bottom rails in 1948. This was because the lateral strength of flat-bottom rails was greater than that of bullhead rails.

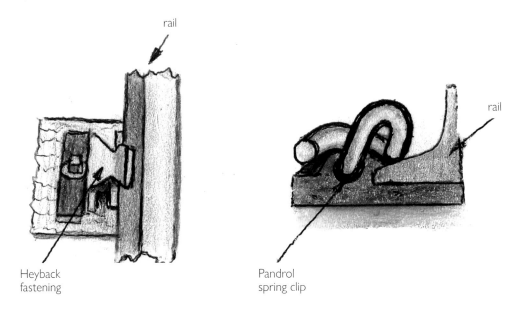

Heyback fastening – track fastening.

Pandrol spring clip – track fastening.

Experience running high-speed trains during the 1930s showed that bullhead rails could not cope without high maintenance costs. By 1948, sophisticated rail fixings for flat-bottom tracks had become available.

CHANGE IN THE RAILWAY SYSTEM

There have been great changes in the railway system since the end of steam-hauled trains in 1968 (except for special trains and heritage railways). Passenger coaches have become heavier, and passenger speeds have increased considerably. Freight traffic has changed dramatically. Up until the 1960s, many trains were not fitted with continuous brakes and consisted of loose-coupled four-wheeled wagons. Freight was often in pick-up goods trains, picking up and dropping off wagons at wayside stations, which were much more numerous than they are now. The brakes could only be applied from the guard's van and the locomotive when the train was in motion. Longer distance freight trains were the precursors of modern freight trains, having continuous brakes.

Modern freight trains impose very high longitudinal forces when coming to a halt. The vehicles all have brakes and can travel at 125km/h (78mph). Trackwork, ballast depths and formations have all had to change and adapt to the much higher static and dynamic loadings that are features of the modern railway system.

Of course, material technologies have played a major part in the development of the railway system. As train speeds have increased, so has the need for more durable materials and technologies. Materials have had to be developed to cope with the increased speeds and greater loads. Back in 1857, the then Midland Railway started laying steel rails to replace the wrought-iron rails then in use. In one location the new steel rails lasted sixteen years, when previously the rails on the site had to be replaced every few months!

All aspects of railway construction play a part in safety. For example, effective drainage on track formations is very important. In the early days of railways, drainage was sometimes neglected, through ignorance, and a number of major accidents are known to have been caused by this factor.

THE DYNAMICS OF TRAIN MOTION

A great deal of attention was given to the study of the dynamic behaviour of trains when they were in motion, particularly at speed. It was found that by raising the

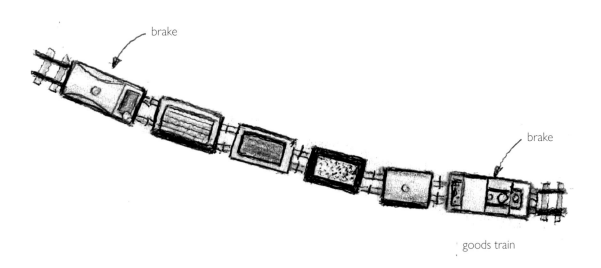

brake

brake

goods train

Pick-up goods train, with brakes only in the brake van and engine.

Superelevation – to balance the effective weights on inner and outer wheels.

superelevation or cant to
balance the weights on the
two wheels on a curve

outer rails on curves, by amounts that depend on the line speed, curve radius and train weight, the chances of trains derailing became less. Raising the outer rails above the inner rails was known as 'superelevation', or in railway terminology, 'adding cant to the rails'.

FORCES THAT GOVERN THE PHYSICAL BEHAVIOUR OF RAILS

There has also been a growing understanding of forces that govern the physical behaviour of rails. For example, as a train goes round a curve, two force systems act on it. The first involves forces that ensure that a railway vehicle follows the curve of the rails, the most important being on the outer leading wheel. These 'guiding forces' are more related to train interaction with the track, rather than speed. The second force system concerns centrifugal force, and it is this force that is principally what the cant (superelevation) is designed to neutralize. We can experience centrifugal force on fast revolving fairground rides, but the thrills that these give us are not quite what we want on our everyday train journeys!

Actually, although the high speed behaviour of trains on curves has gained most attention, the combination of guiding forces and centrifugal force rarely reach a point where they are great enough in relation to the weight on a railway vehicle's wheels for derailments to happen.

Railway wheelsets are coned, as an antidote to what are known as creepage forces. If a wheelset moves laterally towards one rail, the wheel diameter it is sitting on increases in size as it moves across the rail. The wheel on the other line, as part of the wheelset, moves across but is sitting on the smaller diameter part of the wheel. This movement causes creepage forces, which try to return the wheels to their original positions – in the track centre.

The return movement of the wheels can sometimes overshoot the centre and then return the other way with a see-saw movement. This oscillatory behaviour depends on the cone angle of the wheel – too shallow, and this interferes with its ability to guide the wheel back to the centre, too steep and the wheel will 'hunt' across the track. Energy is absorbed into the system via creepage and oscillation can grow, only being stopped by flange contact with the rail.

RAIL BEHAVIOUR UNDER PRESSURE

When a wheel runs along a rail with its flange away from the corner ('gauge corner') of the rail, the contact area is extremely small. In fact theoretically, contact between the wheel and the rail is only possible at a point. An infinitely large pressure would be needed where the two touched. Actually, both surfaces deform a little, and a 'contact patch' is created where they meet. The maximum area is around 100mm². Under the wheels, the pressure is very great indeed: with a vehicle of considerable weight, it is in fact greater than the yield point of steel, and causes plastic behaviour of the steel near the contact point. The metal under the wheel would be squeezed out sideways if it wasn't prevented from doing so by the rest of the metal in the rail. In fact the metal on the rail-head surface does move because of the intense pressure and the forces along the plane of the rail. This can be seen and is very marked when the curves are sharp and trains move slowly.

WHEEL BEHAVIOUR ON RAILS

The study of wheel behaviour on rails shows that when a wheel turns, it will move slightly more than the distance it should have done. If a brake were applied, movement would be slightly less than it should have been. These fractional increases or decreases are known as creepage. Creepage is caused by plastic deformations on a microscopic scale in the area of the contact patch, when wheels are moved under traction or brakes.

TRANSITION CURVES

If a train is approaching a curved section of track from a straight section, there will obviously be a sudden motional change where the train enters the curve. To avoid this situation, a 'transition' curve is needed, gradually changing its radius from the straight track to match the radius of the curved section.

The simplest way to approach actually using a transition curve is to imagine having a straight length of tracks followed by a constant radius curve, and creating a new transition curve to replace the straight length of track. The existing curve will need to be 'shifted', as shown in the diagrams. To lay out the new arrangement, either the straight or curve has to be 'shifted' to a parallel position. Just easing a curve by changing the centre to a wider radius causes a sharper radius to be needed in at least one of the curves feeding the fake transition. An arrangement for a transition curve can be seen from the diagrams.

VERSINES AND CHORDS

If you draw a line across a circle and then draw another line from the centre of that line at right angles to the circle, this line is called a versine; the first line is called a chord.

Versines have been used a great deal in mapping out and planning railways, and also in designing track formations. A versine varies inversely with the radius of a circle: if a circle gets larger, its versine gets smaller.

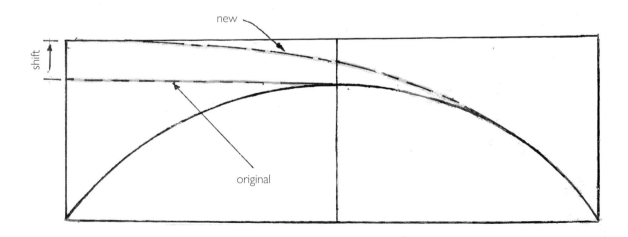

Adding a transition curve.

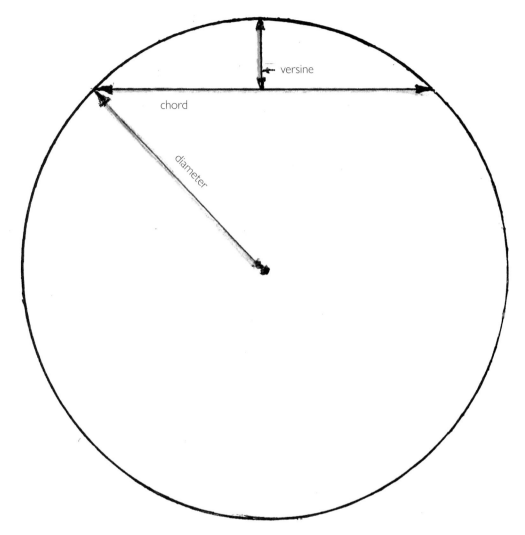

Constructing a versine.

If you know the length of a versine and the chord length that goes with it, it is possible to work out the diameter or radius of the circle it is associated with. Even if a curve is of very large radius, if you can measure a versine from it accurately, it is a simple matter to work out that radius without directly measuring it.

Particularly in the days when these things were accomplished manually, permanent way engineers would find out the radius of a curve by this method. Since a versine became shorter the larger the radius of a curve became, this kind of operation was manageable.

Transition curves also have an inverse relationship to radii. Where a transition curve meets a straight, the effective radius is infinitely large, but as the curve opens out, the effective radius at each point along its length becomes smaller until it coincides with the main track curve.

WORKING OUT A TRANSITION CURVE

Nowadays, a form of curve known as a clothoid is used to derive the shape of transition curves. In the past, a cubic parabola was used. A clothoid curve evolves to become a spiral form. A cubic parabola is very similar over the first portion of its curve, but is not able to turn more than a right angle. Since we are most interested in the first part of the curve, in modelling terms, the cubic parabola is probably the most useful as it is easier to work out and apply.

Returning to the example of changing a length of straight track to a transition curve leading to a curve of constant radius, notice the chord across the curve. A versine runs vertically from the centre of the chord, and the line continues, crossing the 'shift'. The versine equals three times the 'shift' distance, and the transition curve passes exactly through the centre of the 'shift'. Notice that the transition curve is measured along the tangent (along the top horizontal line of the diagram). There is a difference between the length as measured along the curve, and the length along the tangent, which the clothoid calculation takes

into account; in calculations for the cubic parabola they are assumed to be the same. Nevertheless, the inaccuracies involved in the latter are only small.

Of course, one object of a transition curve is to allow the canted outside rail of a curve to climb gradually rather than suddenly. Where there is no transition, the maximum allowable speed on a full size railway is based on the concept of a virtual transition.

A VIRTUAL TRANSITION
A vehicle travelling along a straight track at a uniform velocity will experience a change when it enters a curve, where it starts to have angular momentum. The change of motion will continue until the vehicle is fully on the curve, after which it will move with constant angular momentum. The change in motion of the vehicle from straight to curved conditions is said to represent a virtual transition.

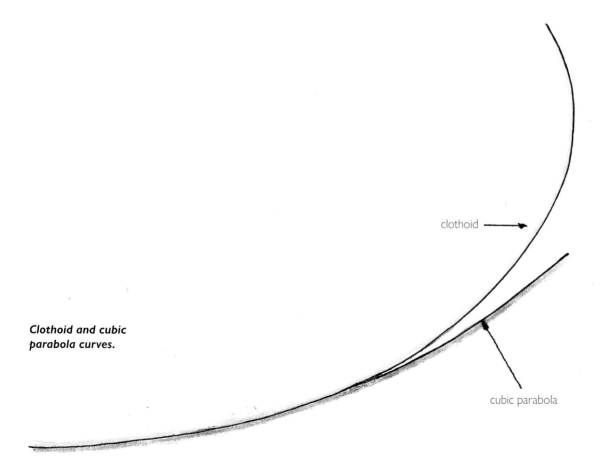

Clothoid and cubic parabola curves.

clothoid

cubic parabola

TURNOUTS AND CROSSINGS

In railway terminology 'plain line' is the term given to open stretches, or railway with one direction of travel. Often, however, one line will need to cross or to join with another line, and this is done with an arrangement of 'switches and crossings'. These arrangements can be very complex in order to cope with different arrangements of trackwork, but they are made to suit these two requirements singly or in combination: the need for one track to cross, or to join another.

Model railways sometimes use different terminology. A 'point' is a turnout that in prototype railway language consists of switches and a crossing. A 'crossing' enables a wheel travelling along a rail to pass through the rail of a track that crosses it. Switches enable a vehicle to be diverted from one line to another. Each turnout has a set of switches that control two switch rails and two stock rails.

COMMON CROSSINGS

The crossing element is known as a 'common crossing' because there are far more acute crossings of this type

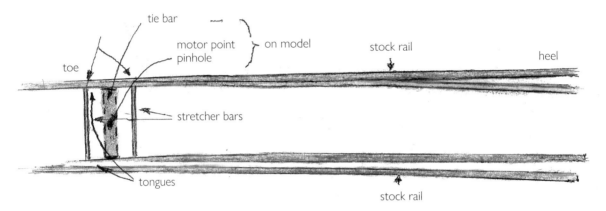

A PAIR OF SWITCHES

Common crossing with a pair of switches.

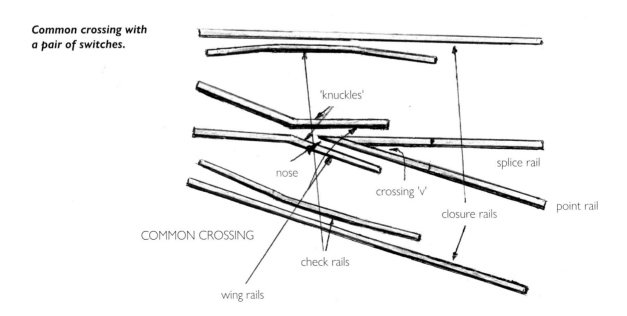

COMMON CROSSING

than obtuse crossings. Every turnout has an acute crossing. In the plain crossing situation, where two lines cross each other, there are two types: square track crossings and obtuse crossings, usually known as diamond crossings.

At the theoretical intersection point, where two lines meet, in the common crossing, the point rail doesn't finish in a sharp point, but is cut back to end in what is known as a 'blunt nose'. The theoretical point is known as the 'fine point'.

> **SAFETY**
>
> **The majority of modern turnouts have switch heaters to keep the switches operating in cold weather. Electric point machines have an electric motor, a drive mechanism, a detector mechanism that can detect the position of the switches, and the lock device, which is designed to retain the closed rail strongly to its associated stock rail.**

FACING POINTS

Earlier in railway history, facing turnouts were avoided on passenger lines because of the high risk of accidents due to poor track standards, and because high safety standards could not be maintained. Facing crossovers were particularly avoided. Up and down lines, with trains travelling in different directions to one another, on crossovers set the wrong way, resulted in horrific consequences. Looking at track plans of old stations, it is apparent how far the railway companies went to avoid this sort of situation. On modern railways there are a great many facing points, maintained by sophisticated control and locking devices.

MORE ABOUT TURNOUTS

A turnout is what the name suggests: one track turns out from another. Each turnout has two switches. There are two movable rails called switch rails, which select the direction of travel of a vehicle through the

turnout. The two rails are machined (planed) to be tapered at one end. The tapered section is called the switch tongue, and this fits snugly against the stock rail: when held in this position, a wheel moves smoothly from one rail to the other.

The thinned end of each switch rail is usually called the toe; while the switch rail on one side of the turnout is held firmly against the stock rail, the rail next to it, the switch rail on the other side of the turnout is held away from the stock rail. This allows the wheel not being guided to follow a different path and to pass through undisturbed.

The point where a stock rail is connected to the plain line following it, is called a 'stock-rail joint'. If a through track through the turnout is straight, one of the stock rails will also be straight.

THE GEOMETRY OF TURNOUTS

Basically, there are two types of modern standard turnout: natural angle turnouts and composite turnouts. The simplest geometric type of turnout is the natural angle turnout. This consists of a segment of a circle for the diverging curved line, which begins in a tangent with the through line and ends in a tangent to the straight line of the crossing. In a composite turnout, the radius of the switch curve is different to the turnout curve. Either can be longer or shorter than the other, and sometimes these involve a transition curve.

Transition curves are used in place of natural angle and composite turnouts for running lines through crossovers. Transition curves reduce the effect of a sudden change of direction on passenger comfort. Transitions are regarded as a special type of composite turnout.

In this chapter we have looked a little at the history of railway tracks. We have also considered the forces that the track is subject to, and how it is configured to deal with them. The basics of turnouts have been described, and the subject will be considered in more detail later in the book, both in terms of modern railways and those of the steam age.

I've mentioned superelevation and transition curves, which are important to prototype railways. Are these really necessary on a model railway? Superelevation (cant) doesn't appear too often on model railways, or maybe if it is present, its visual effect is too subtle to be noticed. It is perhaps worthwhile on layouts with fine scale trackwork, where track and wheel standards are very close to scaled-down versions of the real thing. But in general terms model railways run perfectly well without it.

The use of transitional curves is worthwhile on any layout, and makes an enormous difference to the look of a layout. In fact, an oval layout with what might be seen as 'toy train' track will look a lot less so with a few larger radius curves added, even if the result is not truly a transition. In an old book on prototype track I have, it mentions that almost any kind of transition is better than none at all!

MODEL RAILWAY GEOMETRY

The short piece in this book earlier about the geometry of turnouts might appear academic. However, it does apply directly to model railways.

I recently needed to change some of the track on a layout built twenty-five years ago because of damage. I replaced the turnouts, which were Shinohara, with Peco code 75 small-radius ones – the originals were code 70. I traced the outlines of the two types, and they make an interesting comparison. The Peco turnout seems to be a composite type and incorporates a transition curve. Although it is, at a glance, quite similar to the Peco turnout, the Shinohara is of the natural angle type with a constant radius curve from the switch rail to the crossing.

A SOURCE OF TRACK KNOWLEDGE

In researching this book I came across the organization known as 'The Permanent Way Institution', which turned out to be a major force in the world of track engineering and related disciplines. I discovered there were two books by them. One, *Understanding Track Engineering*, was published quite recently; the other, *British Railway Track*, in 1971 – rather surprisingly I found this in a local library! Both books are a mine of information, and I leant equally on information from them in preparing for this book. I am very grateful for these sources being available.

Interestingly, the two books are very different. The older book contains almost a crash course in understanding geometry, starting with basic arithmetic. The second, more recent book assumes a more sophisticated knowledge of maths. Were the two books aimed at slightly different audiences? The older book seems to be pitched at individuals with a practical rather than a formal education background. One wonders whether, in the past, permanent way engineers often worked their way up from the ranks, as it were, whereas nowadays, education to degree standard is probably needed. Modern knowledge of the subject as imparted in the most recent book does involve modern sophisticated scientific concepts, and to understand these properly probably requires a fairly advanced level of understanding of current physics.

CHAPTER TWO

SCALE, GAUGE AND PERSPECTIVE

While I am writing this, glancing across the room, I can see a small replica of an Ancient Egyptian statue of the god Bastet. This has the character of a cat. When we build model railways, we refer to whether a model looks right or wrong according to how much to scale it is. Generally we refer to model scales as ratios. So, for example, the scale of 00 gauge is 4mm = 1 or 1/76 scale, or 1:76, where each linear dimension of a prototype object will be 76 × the size of the model dimensions.

DEFINING GAUGE

A gauge is usually a plain measurement. For example, most British railways have track laid to 4ft 8½in gauge, but track gauges can be wider or narrower than this. Gauges can define other measurements besides track gauges, which always refer to the distances between the insides of the rail heads. Another type of railway gauge is loading gauge, which defines the overall dimensions of railway vehicles so that they can pass through tunnels and over bridges, and clear the edges of platforms.

It is not hard for gauges and scales to be confused with one another. For example, 009-gauge narrow-gauge vehicles are to 4mm scale, but run on the same track

STANDARD GAUGE

According to the Permanent Way Institutions book *Understanding Track Engineering*, around 60 per cent of current railways are standard gauge (4ft 8½in). Hardly a universal standard!

as N gauge (2mm scale). The term '00' is commonly used to describe a gauge – 00 gauge – but it is also used to describe a scale, as in '00 scale'. Actually, in 4mm scale, which is the same as 00 scale, the principal British track gauge (standard gauge) scales up as 4ft 1½in, not 4ft 8½in, which it ought to be – quite a significant difference. Because of the peculiar history of British model railways, 16.5mm gauge came to be 00 gauge – the gauge of 4mm scale.

Another scale uses a 16.5mm track gauge called HO, which has a scale of 3.5mm equalling 1ft. Being a slightly smaller size, the scale discrepancy when modelling 4ft 8½in gauge is less than that in 4mm scale. HO scale is the major scale for most continental modellers, and also those in the USA. In general, most HO (3.5mm scale) modellers are happy with 16.5mm as a gauge because it is reasonably close to what it should be. However, the situation in 4mm scale is rather different.

Many years ago, a new gauge was created, of 18.2mm known as EM gauge, which for standard gauge is more accurate than 00. Some modellers later looked into the possibility of an even more accurate track gauge of 18.83mm, with associated finer wheel standards. This is known as P4.

The market for commercial ready-to-run systems is greater for HO scale using 16.5mm gauge as a track gauge, even though quite a few British modellers use the same gauge calling it 00, and model in 4mm scale rather than 3.5mm scale (HO).

Because of the greater market available for HO, most track systems are made for a scale of 3.5mm equalling 1ft (HO), and not 4mm scale (00), although the gauge is the same. British 4mm-scale trains are run on 3.5mm-scale tracks because that is what is available – though the track looks fine in itself, because

*Egyptian cat
god effigy.*

it is made to a consistent scale and gauge relative to HO scale, and the gauge is consistent too, relative to that of the track. However, because 4mm-scale trains are made to a slightly larger scale, the track is a little under scale, relatively. Of course there is an argument that because most track layouts are very restricted in space, the slightly smaller scale track gives layouts a more spacious feel.

So we have 00 trains running on HO track. What tends to emphasize, usually, the fact that the track is a little too narrow, when running 4mm-scale (00) trains, is the slightly greater overhang of each vehicle on each side. Of course this doesn't really show if the train is viewed sideways on. It is more visible when trains are seen from the front, as can be the case on a circular, continuous layout – though when a train is moving, the overhang tends to be less obvious.

How did 00 and HO trains end up sharing the same track gauge? It all goes back to the 1920s. Previously, 0 gauge (7mm = 1 foot) was the smallest commercial

gauge, though smaller working trains had been produced. In 1921 W.G. Bassett-Lowke, a principal model railway manufacturer, produced a series of train sets designed in England but made in Germany. These were built to half '0' scale, and the dimensions were in keeping with the British loading gauge in this size. The train sets were mass produced and proved to be very popular. Trains in this scale were quickly christened HO (half 0). But Bassett-Lowke called his systems '00' gauge!

According to E.W. Twining – a friend of Bassett-Lowke and a manufacturer in his own right – 4mm scale was adopted to create space so that more powerful mechanisms could be fitted to the locos. The half '0' gauge (HO) of 16.5mm was kept, though the scale was increased to 4mm from 3.5mm = 1ft. The reason given for this was that because British locomotives were smaller than continental locos, fitting the motors then available was not practical, especially in smaller prototypes. When Hornby entered the market, adopting a scale of 4mm to the foot and the 16.5mm gauge in

An unusual setting for a model railway.
A Selsey tramway train skirts Pagham
harbour, Sussex, now a nature reserve.

the 1930s, the future of 00 gauge in Britain was assured. Curiously, in the USA 00 gauge is 19mm! This gauge was also suggested as a track gauge here, as an alternative to the narrow 16.5 before the war, for 4mm scale.

There are overall a great many scales and gauges in the model railway hobby, and the main ones are listed here. Several gauges can exist in each scale: 4mm scale, for example, covers modelling in standard gauge, also broad gauges, and narrow gauges too.

Some scales and gauges have a great deal of support from the trade, others very little. Sometimes items available for modellers of one gauge/scale are usable by others modelling in different scales and gauges. For example, N-gauge mechanisms are sometimes used as chassis for 4mm narrow-gauge locos, which share the same gauge (4mm) but have larger bodies to 4mm scale, or 3.5mm scale if they are continental or based on US prototypes. Small-gauge full-size prototypes are quite small compared to their standard-gauge counterparts, so some people get confused with models of a smaller scale but replicating bigger vehicles.

I have a layout with both 00-gauge and 009 tracks; both are to 4mm scale, but sometimes the relatively small narrow-gauge trains are assumed to be N gauge, and people ask why I have N-scale trains running on my 00-gauge layout! Of course each scale/gauge combination has its own devoted following. In fact there is nothing to stop anyone creating their own scale/gauge combination, even if they are the only one using it!

If you are working in scales and gauges not directly supported by the trade then you have to be self-reliant. Although motors and gears intended for other scales/gauges might prove useful, and other parts too, it is unusual these days to hear of modellers making their own motors and cutting their own gears. And even when modellers were forced to rely on their own resources, because trade support was fairly minimal, only model engineers tended to do that. In the days when model railways required quite a bit of work on the part of modellers, scratch building was the order of the day. But when someone went to a great deal of trouble to scratch build their own favourite loco or vehicle, it was rather sad if a manufacturer then brought out a model or kit of the prototype.

When I was younger, books and articles often pointed out that the enjoyment to be had from railway

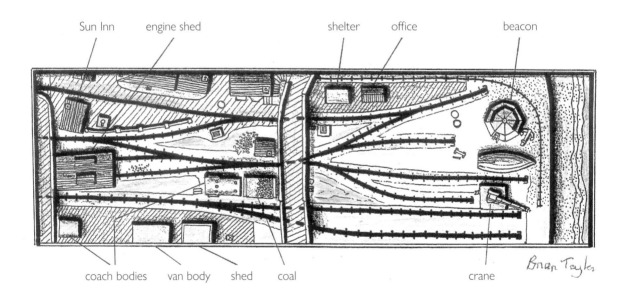

A plan of the author's model layout 'Oystemere', 0-16.5-scale gauge. Large scale but a small layout.

LONE MODELLERS AND STRANGE RAILWAYS

I wonder how many modellers are the only ones following a particular scale/gauge? Of course, monorails could be said to have no gauge at all, and yet they are railways, and so they must have a modelling following. One of the most peculiar railways was the Indian Potalia state monorail tramway. This had road wheels running on a road on one side, and railway wheels running on a single rail on the other! Is there anyone who has modelled this?

ABOVE: Author's sketch of a much simpler harbour layout, taking up even less space.

Bren Taylor

BELOW: Compact 4mm-scale harbour scene.

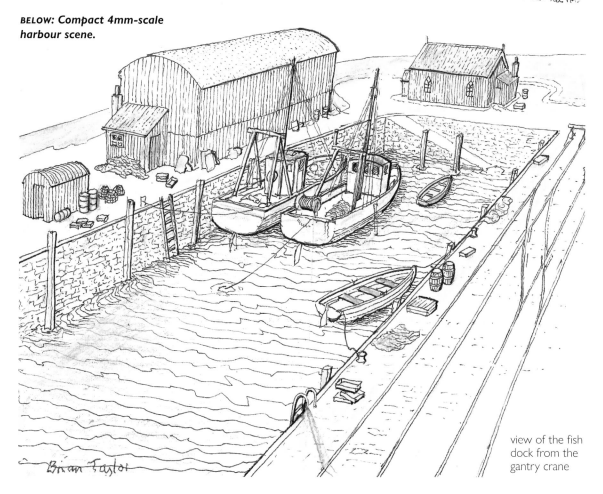

Brian Taylor

view of the fish dock from the gantry crane

modelling was savouring the process, enjoying using the tools, and the satisfaction of a 'good job well done'. There were sayings such as 'more haste, less speed', which, it seemed to me, really meant 'no haste, no speed'; another was 'care now means pride later'. With the benefit of hindsight, I can see that the pundits of the time were right: it is better to savour the experience along the way, rather than rush headlong to finish.

WHAT TO CHOOSE – AND WHY

With so many scales and gauges to choose from, it is better to keep a watch on articles appearing in the model press and see what appeals the most in terms of prototypes and which model to embrace. The following are some of the reasons for making particular choices:

- space available
- availability of commercially available locos and stock
- attractiveness of particular prototypes
- ease of setting up
- relative costs
- size
- nostalgic choice
- domestic situation
- expense

Nostalgia seems to play a big part in what people choose to model, most often based on childhood experiences – though it is quite possible to be nostalgic about railway prototypes that existed before you were even born! For example, I have often modelled the Lynton

A simple narrow-gauge scene. The engine shed is Scottish. The tiny watermill was a Welsh building, in 7mm scale.

Brian Taylor

and Barnstaple railway, which closed many years before my birth. I think I was influenced by the great attractiveness of the prototype, and the fact that it ran through scenery, which really appealed to me.

I know one lady who says she is nostalgic about the times she had with her husband before he had a model railway! I remember seeing quite a few 'I'm a model railway widow' T-shirts. I've heard a number of wives or partners say they have hardly seen their other halves since they had railways…and some are not unhappy about that! I suppose a spouse's obsession with model railways must sometimes have been cited as grounds for a divorce. Actually, wives and partners are generally quite supportive of the hobby – and these days, quite a few join in. In conversation, a rather attractive girl told me she was sure her boyfriend liked his railway more than he did her! But if you can't beat them, join them.

PERSPECTIVE

Before moving on to the design of model railways, there are other factors relating to scale that are worth looking at. Since scale is a fundamental principle of model making, it seems a fixed and immutable quantity: we choose a scale and resolutely adhere to it in any particular situation related to modelling. It is easy to forget that because of the peculiarities of human perception, objects appear to get smaller the further away from our eyes they are. We see things in perspective.

Another factor is that, to some extent, we are able to perceive depth, because we have two eyes, each seeing the world from a slightly different viewpoint. Our brain creates a single composite image, which contains a sense of depth. Interestingly, when we look at a scene in, say, 4mm scale (1:76), the distance between our eyes is effectively seventy-six times greater than the eye spacing of a 4mm figure. Looking at our 4mm-scale scene, our sense of depth must be, to some extent, enhanced. Also, it is clear that our sense of depth must be different when we look at scenes in various scales. Looking at close quarters at a rather nice model of a small shed in 2mm scale, I noticed that I could see both ends of the shed at the same time! This would be impossible looking at a real shed.

MODEL RAILWAY PERSPECTIVE

A line-up of model buildings on a layout will appear in perspective quite naturally, without the buildings being made smaller as they recede into the distance. However, because of the limited depth of baseboards, lines of objects often need to be continued on to the backscene. It is possible to do this, but it is rather difficult to avoid the overall scene looking wrong as the onlooker moves to either side.

To work, perspective on a two-dimensional surface (that is, the backscene) depends on being looked at from one viewpoint. I'll illustrate a way round this problem later on. We'll also look at colour perspective.

To give more of a sense of depth – enhancing the perspective effect – modellers sometimes place models made to a smaller scale towards the rear of the layout. This is fine, as long as trains of a larger scale don't pass near them! If this happens, the perspective effect collapses, and it is generally better to use smaller models of the same scale as the main layout. If large buildings to a smaller scale are necessary, they should be placed behind where the larger-scale trains run, rather than in front. Trains of a smaller scale compared to those in the foreground are fine further back on the layout. Small narrow-gauge trains of the main scale might also work in this situation.

I built a small '00' layout consisting of a small oval track (standard gauge), two sidings, and a station with a single platform. I decided to add a narrow-gauge line to this, and so I carved away the scenery and added the track. I was surprised to find that the layout looked much more spacious with the addition of the new track. In fact this is a good example of our eyes being drawn to follow lines 'unconsciously'. Because the narrow-gauge track wound its way across the layout and back again, it created a longer line for the eyes to follow and made the layout look more spacious than it was before, with just the standard-gauge line.

Roads and rivers can visually have the same effect on a layout. However, it is important for them to pass into a backscene, because without a backscene they appear to fall off the edge of the baseboard! They can appear to pass 'off scene' via a bend hidden by trees, for example, or under a bridge, or behind buildings. The part of our brain that deals with visual things will assume

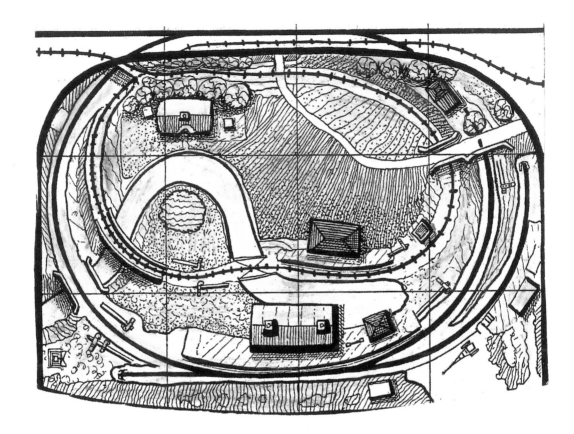

A small layout (4mm scale). The narrow gauge was a later addition: with this the layout looked more expansive, surprisingly.

they have passed from view temporarily, for that is the brain's 'real life' experience of similar situations.

Conjuring tricks are based on persuading the brain that a certain reality is different to what we assume it to be, and to some extent, producing model railways involves a similar illusion. When we look at a very realistic model layout, the part of our brain that determines the actual physical reality, behind the millions of nervous impulses flooding in from our optic nerves, must to some extent be convinced that the scene we are looking at is real. But then, perhaps another part of the brain says 'Ah, but it's a model!' It is easier to be convinced by photos of models as to their reality, because we often can't be sure whether the images are taken from real subjects or not.

As a teenager I remember looking through a friend's collection of *Railway Modeller* magazines. In the October 1960 issue I came across some amazing photographs: I was completely stunned by what I saw, and couldn't believe the photos were of a model. The title of the article was 'Does your railway live?', and the modeller was George Iliffe Stokes – and that article has been a source of inspiration to me since. The photography was excellent, too – it was the work of John Himmens and J.H. Russell, and the pictures just ooze atmosphere. George Iliffe Stokes was well known for his model buildings, and wrote a book that is full of useful information; it was published by Peco and is long out of print, but copies are sometimes available via the internet.

PERSPECTIVE IN PHOTOGRAPHY

A photograph is a true perspective projection. If you photocopy a photograph so that the image is in the centre of a larger piece of paper, the picture can be extended by drawing perspective lines from it. These lines will come together at points on a horizon, and in this way the picture will be shown to obey the rules of perspective.

Of course, most photographs are taken from one viewpoint. Because we observe an image with two eyes – two viewpoints placed a few inches away from each other – looking at a photograph is like looking at a scene with one eye shut: any sense of depth is largely lost, as happens when we close one eye and observe the world. So if we take a photograph of a scene, that photograph will not look the same as the view we would see if we were to stand in the same spot observing the same scene with both eyes open.

On some preserved railways it is possible to stand on a spot where a photographer stood many years ago and looked at much the same scene. An example is Woody Bay station on the Lynton and Barnstaple Railway. It is interesting to compare photographs taken from the same position of essentially the same view, but looked at with both eyes. My feeling is that photographs make the station look longer than it looks in real life. This is probably because our two-eyed view takes in more sideways information than a conventional photo (we are looking at perspective from two viewpoints, and our brain adds the two images together), so the length dimension in a photograph appears more dominant, whilst in the actual view, the apparent width is greater than it might seem.

For example, some years ago, a friend told me that a class 56 diesel loco had derailed near Haywards Heath and was lying on its side at the bottom of an

A Class 56 diesel loco lies on its side at the bottom of an embankment.

embankment. One Sunday afternoon a group of us set off across country to see if we could find the engine. Eventually we broke through some trees and found it. Seeing the big machine at close quarters made a very impressive sight, especially as it was lying on its side. We tried to photograph the scene, but couldn't get the visible part of the whole locomotive in any shot. It struck me that it might be possible to draw the recumbent engine, so I came back the next day with a sketch pad and produced a drawing. Because I was looking at the scene with two eyes, my eyes could take in the whole scene. (The picture later appeared in the *West Sussex Gazette*.)

This is quite a good example of the difference between an ordinary photograph and an actual first-hand view of a scene. The difference between a drawing made of an actual scene, and one made by copying a photo, is also quite marked.

KEEPING A SENSE OF REALISM

I've tried to stress the subjective aspects of building a model railway. Strict adherence to scale has always been regarded as an indispensable first principle of modelling, almost an objective absolute. This is fine, but we often have to compromise, if only to scale down various aspects of prototypes simply just for space considerations. The question is a subjective one: how can we reduce prototypes in size and keep a sense of realism? How can we get away with this gracefully? Most model railways, fine scale or otherwise, represent foliage with areas of ground-up plastic foam, and water with various plastic materials – real water doesn't look too realistic in model form. Buildings are often made of cardboard or plastic sheet – the list is endless. On model railways nothing is quite what it appears to be! It's that subjective sense of realism that ultimately counts. As the old saying goes: 'If it looks right, it is right.'

MORE ABOUT PERSPECTIVE

Further to our observations concerning perspective, it might be said that basically there are two types of perspective: linear and aerial.

LINEAR PERSPECTIVE

We all know that objects appear to get smaller with distance. If we consider a figure standing in the distance, and imagine a line from the top of its head to an eye (the centre of the eye) and another line from the feet to the centre of the eye, the angle between the two lines will become smaller the further the figure moves away from the eye. The size of the image of the figure on the retina of the eye will depend on the angle: the smaller the angle between the two lines from the figure's extremities (the feet and the top of head), the smaller the image on the eye.

If the figure carries on moving away from the eye, the image on the retina will get so small that it effectively vanishes. If our figure is moving away along the centre of a road that is straight and always the same width, the road will appear to get narrower with distance until the edges converge to a point. This will be the same point as that of the figure. This is the vanishing point.

Single-Point Perspective

Let us look at a building in perspective. One way of drawing objects in perspective is to use single-point perspective. Here one side is drawn exactly as it would be in reality, as if we were looking straight at it. The lines of the other visible sides, however, converge to a vanishing point. It is best to use a single-point perspective near to the interface between the baseboard and the backscene, because the eye and the brain are more tolerant to off-axis views when images are in single-point perspective.

Two-Point Perspective

If the building is swung round so the onlooker is no longer looking directly at one wall of the building, the horizontal lines of the wall will then converge to a vanishing point. This is an example of two-point perspective. If a line is drawn between the vanishing points of the two walls, this is the horizon line.

AERIAL, OR COLOUR PERSPECTIVE

One form of perspective that is sometimes overlooked is aerial perspective. Light waves travelling through the air are subject to its effects, even down to dust in

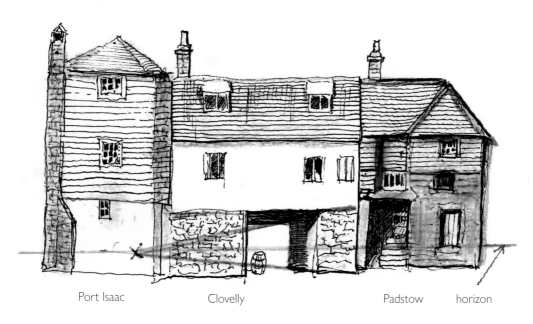

Port Isaac   Clovelly   Padstow   horizon

Single-point perspective. A view of three West Country buildings in single-point perspective, with a low horizon.

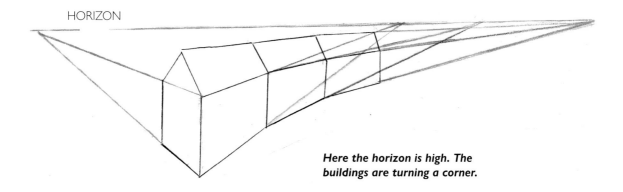

HORIZON

Here the horizon is high. The buildings are turning a corner.

the atmosphere. One very familiar effect is where the yellow part of the light spectrum becomes lost over a distance, and far-off green hills become blue. When viewed close to, colours will appear stronger, while those in the distance appear progressively weaker,

and detail will appear less apparent. By deliberately choosing colours and tones we can create or enhance these effects.

Yellow-green through yellows and oranges to orange-red are known as warm colours. Intensely

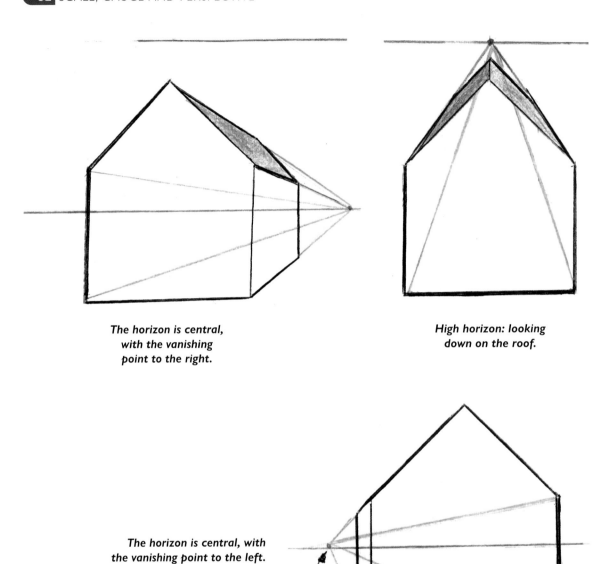

*The horizon is central,
with the vanishing
point to the right.*

*High horizon: looking
down on the roof.*

*The horizon is central, with
the vanishing point to the left.*

warm colours seem to leap towards the viewer. Blue-green through blues and purples are called cool colours, and these seem to recede into the distance.

To use colours in perspective, vivid and intense colours are used in the foreground, with reducing intensity of colours and detail towards the rear of a layout. If you paint an object brilliant red and place it at the back of a layout, it will seem to leap forwards. Colours lose their strength when grey is added, or if they are lightened. This treatment used on buildings and other items can enhance a sense of perspective.

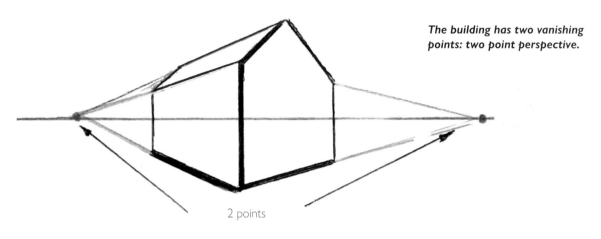

The building has two vanishing points: two point perspective.

2 points

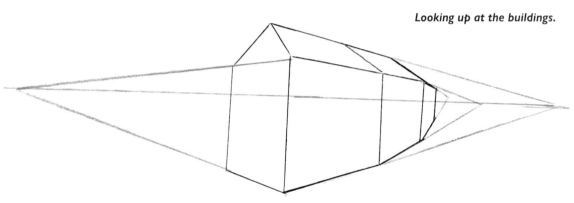

Looking up at the buildings.

The author's layout 'Oystemere'. The backscenes help to convey a sense of distance. The horizon is low.

PECO STUDIO

The author's layout 'Oystemere'. The backscene again helps to convey a sense of distance, with a low horizon.
PECO STUDIO

TALYLLLYN LAKE 0–16.5

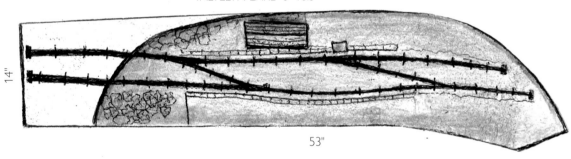

14"

53"

Talyllyn lake layout plan.

OPPOSITE PAGE:
TOP: *Painted backscene of mountains and lakes.*

INSET: *Loco Dolgoch and a lone pony trekker at the lake end.*

BOTTOM: *Track Peco 0–16.5.*

Cast kit water tank.

The ballast up to the sleeper tops is covered in green scenic materials in places.

CHAPTER THREE

LAYOUT, DESIGN, PLANNING AND WHERE TO PUT A LAYOUT

BASIC LAYOUTS

In general, there are three types of model railway, and most layouts are mixtures of these three types.

Layout Type 1:
- The layout is based on nowhere in particular…
- … and no period in particular.
- Running trains is the main objective – as many as possible at one time.
- Scenery is not an important consideration.
- Where there is scenery, it is very basic.
- Sectional track is used.
- The track is not ballasted or painted.

Layout Type 2:
- The layout is based on an actual place…
- and is set in a particular time period.
- Locos and rolling stock are correct for that place and period.
- The layout is operated to a particular period working timetable.
- It has working signals, correct in type and position…
- … and 'fine-scale' track, ballasted and painted.
- The layout would be built to a correct plan derived from prototype maps and plans…
- … and would be a scaled-down replica of a prototype railway scene – scaled down with as little compromise as possible.

Layout Type 3
- Based on the concept of producing a 3D picture or a railway location replicating the 'atmosphere' of the original.
- The layout makes use of 'illusion', using visual tricks in the way that a figurative artist can portray a scene in two dimensions or a 3D scene.
- The layout is based on scale but with modified dimensions where needed, to give the best overall effect in the space available.

THE BACKSCENE

The backscene often plays an important part in a diorama, and can be used to extend the visual space of a model. The diorama approach is more common in other forms of modelling – such as in military modelling – but it is applicable to model railways. Many model railways show a mixture of the different approaches above, while modellers are often inspired by the concepts of the second type of model railway layout, which can be very effective where space is available. Unfortunately, to portray a full-size railway location to scale is out of the question for many modellers, since in most households the space available for a model railway is limited. Hence the popularity of small branch-line terminus layouts!

Of course we are all children at heart, and how many of us can resist the sight of a model train chasing its tail around an oval of track? For some modellers, watching trains run is enough in itself to give them great satisfaction. However, modelling railways to exacting standards can also be very satisfying in itself, and some modellers are quite happy just building models without too much concern about when the trains will run. The model railway hobby is certainly a very 'broad church' – as the saying goes: 'To each his own.'

DESIGNING A LAYOUT

A great many plans for model railways appear in magazines and books, so there is plenty of choice when it comes to choosing a layout plan. To me, part of the fun of building a layout is in planning it. If you are just embarking on putting together your first layout, obviously you will probably rely on other modellers' expertise in terms of layout design, and this is fine. However, you will still need to convert whatever layout plan you choose into something to follow when you are laying out the track and pointwork on the baseboard.

You can, of course, buy the points you need and the flexible track lengths of sections of set track necessary, and lay these out on the board or boards in a 'try it and see' fashion. Alternatively, firms such as Peco provide full-size photocopies of their items of trackwork, which can be used in the same fashion. If you use the actual points and track sections, then these are in the right places when you come to fixing down the track – when you are happy that the track plan works in practice.

SQUARING UP A PLAN

If you want some kind of master plan drawn full size on the board, the easiest way to achieve this is to divide up the original scale plan into squares and mark out squares on the baseboard, suitably in areas and in size. This has the advantage that when the drawing is transferred to the baseboard, guided by the squares, the scenic elements can be marked on the board showing how much space is available for these.

Where cast or kit buildings are to be used, it is useful to draw up outline drawings from the dimensions quoted in the kit instruction sheets or in the company's publicity material. The shapes can then be cut out and placed on the board. A mixture of these methods can be used for trying out the track plan full size and establishing, as much as is possible, the eventual positions of tracks plus scenic elements.

DESIGNING YOUR OWN LAYOUT

Before designing a layout, it is important to know the size of the space or spaces you have at your disposal. If you have only a few feet available, it might be better not to contemplate building a model of Clapham Junction. It is essential that key members of the household are amenable to your plans, or even aware of them. I remember talking to one individual who declared that he intended to build a model of Reading station (which is big). He mentioned that he had fifteen suitable locos, but when I suggested that he might need more, his wife, who had previously been silent, announced in a stentorian voice: 'You will never have more than fifteen trains!' – and the conversation ended there. Later I received a letter from this person saying that after due consideration he and his wife had decided that there would not be a model of Reading station as they had better things to spend their money on!

Funny though this incident was, one can see why the lady reacted as she did, because when the extent of the Reading station model plans were disclosed during our discussion, it was evident that her husband's ideas were mostly news to her. Actually, I have noticed

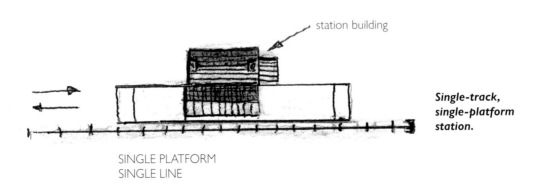

station building

SINGLE PLATFORM
SINGLE LINE

Single-track, single-platform station.

that although many people start off with a notion of building a highly complex main-line station, after a few years of building model railways as a hobby their plans become less extravagant, and they often end up building a simple branch-line terminus.

LAYOUT DESIGN ELEMENTS

BRANCH-LINE LAYOUT

The simplest kind of branch-line terminus consists of a single line ending in a buffer stop and a platform. In terms of steam trains, this type of station is only usable by push-pull – sometimes known as 'pull & push' – trains, which, though having a steam loco at one end, can be driven from both ends of the train. There is a driver's compartment in the last carriage with the necessary controls for the driver to operate the train from there.

Single-car diesel vehicles can also be used with the single platform station, as can multiple-unit trains. Most surviving branch-line terminus stations consist of a platform and a single line.

Run-Round Loop

In the past, this type of station would have had a run-round loop to allow a loco to be disconnected from the first carriage and 'run round' the train, and coupled to the other end of it. This required two points and an extra line forming the loop. Most stations had good facilities, which consisted of one or more sidings, a siding being a section of single track ending in a buffer stop.

Bay Platform

There was sometimes a 'bay' platform, a siding that was laid alongside the opposite side of the platform. Passengers could join or leave a train from either side of the platform. The word 'platform' is confusing because it can refer to a single platform with two platform faces. The two sides would usually be known as platforms one and two, even though there was only one physical platform. A platform also referred to the physical structure.

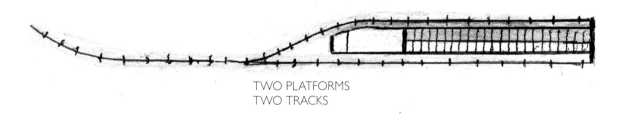

TWO PLATFORMS
TWO TRACKS

The station has two platform faces and two tracks.

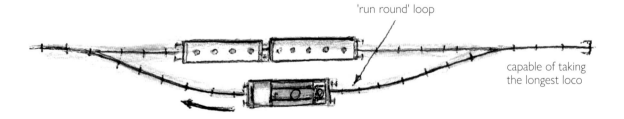

'run round' loop

capable of taking the longest loco

'Running round' a train.

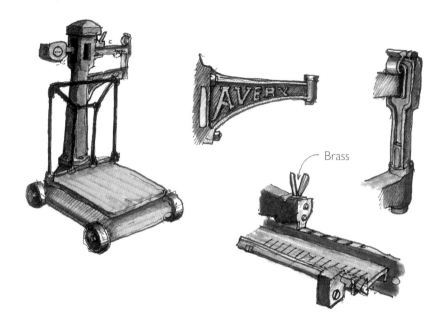

LEFT: Platform weighing machine and details.

Brass

BELOW: Luggage trolley and details – three-wheel design.

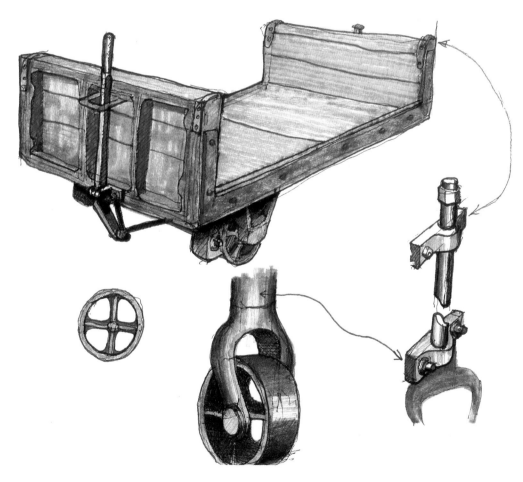

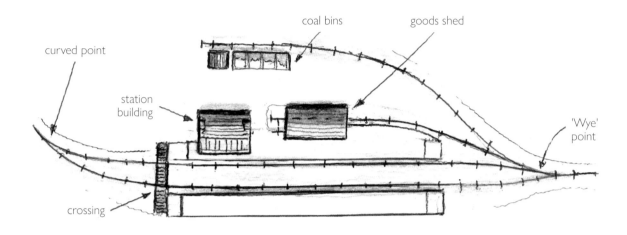

Single-line station with two platforms; trains can pass each other here.

Goods Siding

The station's goods siding would be served by wagons that could be loaded or unloaded from alongside. For example, coal would often be unloaded into coal bins. Coal merchants would frequently operate from a station goods yard and have their own office. Sometimes a goods shed would be constructed by the railway companies to provide covered accommodation to load and unload goods. Quite often a hand crane could be found inside a shed, and sometimes there would be one alongside a siding.

Livestock

Livestock was unloaded and loaded from platforms fenced in to form pens. Sometimes these pens were provided with a separate road for access beside the station approach road, so that passengers could avoid stepping in cowpats! Sometimes the doors of the goods sheds were shut to keep out the wind. A man I knew once told me how he was working in a goods shed one day with the doors closed and suddenly an 'N' class Southern loco crashed through the closed doors!

Sometimes cattle were herded along roads to markets some way from the goods yard. The number of cattle being driven along a road was occasionally

phoned through from a market to the station so the clerks could make up the paperwork in advance – but on some occasions the cattle stampeded, took a wrong turning and ended up miles away, and had to be loaded at a goods yard down the line. But the paperwork had already been prepared and sent off, with, of course, the wrong station recorded on the documents!

Loco Facilities

Some stations had loco facilities, some just had water available via a water crane fed from tanks. Sometimes coal platforms or stages were provided for coaling locos. Even engine sheds were built to protect locos at branch-line termini. Usually an inspection pit was provided.

Signal Boxes

Small signal boxes could be seen on branches, though signalling was often quite rudimentary. Weighbridges were also provided at many branch locations. Another familiar feature would have been a loading gauge: these were built to check whether vehicles had sufficient clearance to pass under bridges and through tunnels. Similar features would also be seen on important lines.

LEFT: Fence connection to a bridge.

BELOW: Fence connection to a bridge with a gate.

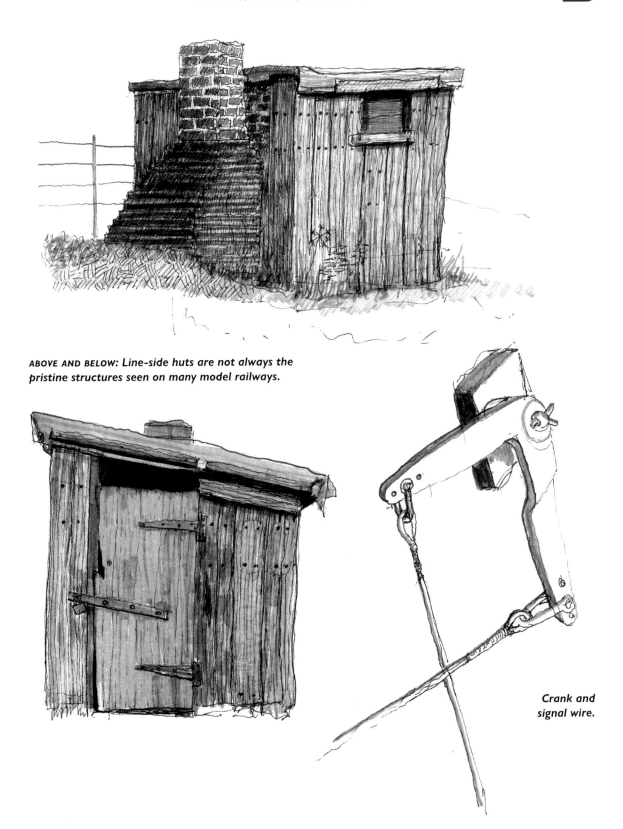

ABOVE AND BELOW: Line-side huts are not always the pristine structures seen on many model railways.

Crank and signal wire.

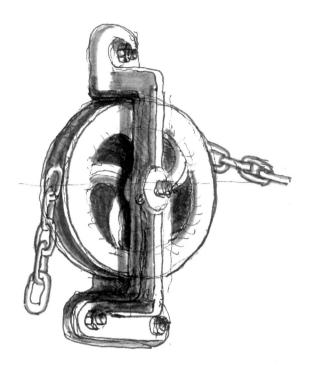

Similar arrangement with a pulley wheel and a chain instead of wires.

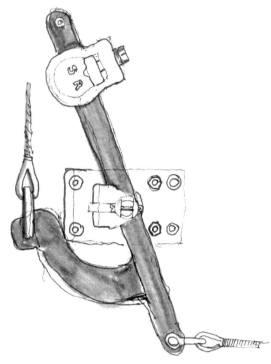

This arrangement has a movable weight.

THE IDEAL PROTOTYPE TO MODEL

Whilst many branch lines were single track, lines serving more important destinations were double track, even four tracked. Some of these branch lines were initially single track, and were converted to double track, an example being the Somerset and Dorset (S&D) line. This was an interesting railway for many reasons, and traffic could be heavy, particularly on summer Saturdays when trains carrying holidaymakers from the North headed to Bournemouth for a week's holiday. Many of the trains needed to be double-headed to pull the long trains over the Mendips. Most goods trains had a banking engine at the rear to help lift the heavy trains over the largely 1-in-50 gradients.

The railway was much loved by enthusiasts because of the number of different loco types to be seen. Former LMS engines were often in evidence, even at Bournemouth West station, the station terminus of

the line in the middle of Southern territory. The most important train was 'The Pines Express', which ran to Manchester. I've included a track plan of Midsomer Norton, one of the S&D stations; quite a lot of traffic passed through here. The S&D station buildings were particularly attractive. Nearby was Norton Hill colliery.

A SIMPLE STATION PLAN

Strangely, Midsomer Norton's track plan is quite rudimentary, with just two goods sidings and two crossovers between the main lines. As a model railway station, Midsomer Norton, following prototype practice, is an interesting station with plenty of operating potential. The trackwork on a model railway doesn't have to be complex to be fascinating to operate.

I've also included a plan of Midford, another S&D location. Double track ended here, just before single-platformed Midford station. Trains travelling north would run on to single-track section, but would sometimes have to reverse back into the layby siding and wait for a southbound train to pass. The manoeuvre involved a very interesting signal, a backing signal: officially this was called a 'wrong road signal', and it permitted the train to reverse. Shortly beyond Midford station was a tunnel followed by Midford goods yard.

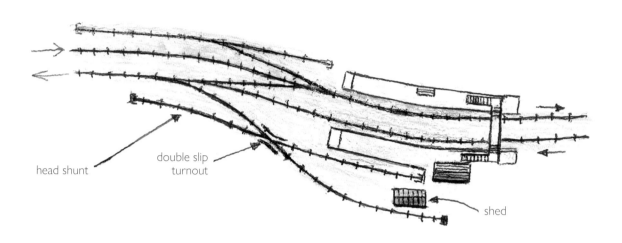

head shunt

double slip turnout

shed

Double-track station with a layby siding. A goods train can 'set back' into this to allow a faster train to pass.

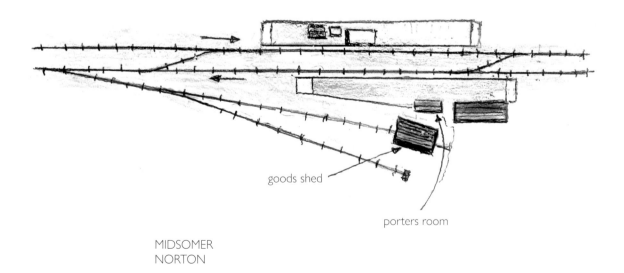

goods shed

porters room

MIDSOMER
NORTON

Midsomer Norton: a double-track station with two sidings and two crossovers.

Midford station was actually situated on the side of a hill. The tunnel was interesting because it was very short, and there was little above the tunnel mouth. These two features made it rather like a toy train-set tunnel. They say there is a prototype for everything! The 'tunnel' was officially known as 'Long Arch Bridge' and was 34m (37yd) long.

It can be seen that on the drawing of Midsomer Norton station, the connections between the two running lines were of the trailing variety. The two lines would have been strictly segregated into up and down lines, and trains could not be accidently switched to a wrong line. The only way to go from one line to the other was by backing the trains across the crossovers. Because of modern safety devices fitted to points (turnouts) and fail-safe signalling, this precaution is no longer regarded as necessary, and trains often travel on what would have been regarded as 'wrong line' working. When designing a model railway track layout, this difference must be taken into account.

I have travelled on four-track main lines where the train followed the inside line track, then moved to the next one in, and so on until the outer line was reached – whereupon the train was switched to follow a diverging track. Previously the lines would have been segregated with, usually, the two outer lines being slow lines, one for each direction. The two inner tracks carried up and down fast trains in the same manner.

Headshunt Line

As already mentioned, Midsomer Norton station was quite basic in terms of its track layout. The S&D was closed during the era of Dr Beeching, but the station has now been preserved and brought back to life. I have included here a number of sketches of station layouts – the one from a two-track line is fairly typical. The sidings came off a line known as a headshunt. Freight locos could move up and down, shunting wagons from one side to another and rearranging them into a different order. This could be accomplished without the loco venturing on to the main running lines, except if it was necessary to 'run round' the train. Stations on the Bluebell Railway were similar to this – even the single-platformed Barcombe station had a headshunt.

'Y' Points

Of course, the complexity of track layouts was very much related to how much traffic they were likely to carry. Quite a simple track layout is that of Northiam station on the Kent and East Sussex Light Railway. The passing loop has 'Y' points, which enable the two lines to 'turnout' from one another more rapidly than if ordinary left or right points are used. For example, in the Peco Streamline ranges (00) of points, the turnout angle is 12.5 degrees. This is also the case with the Y points in the range, except that both sides of the

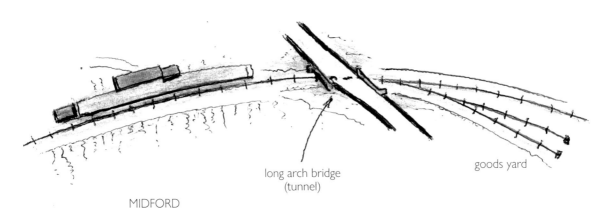

long arch bridge
(tunnel)

goods yard

MIDFORD

Midford station. A single-line station with its goods yard situated on the other side of an adjacent short tunnel.

points are turning out at 12.5 degrees. With Y points the loop can be longer for a given length.

Terminus Turntable

Occasionally, instead of pointwork at the end of a loop, at a terminus a small turntable was used. This was able to move the train engine across to the appropriate line, and also turn it. An Irish narrow-gauge railway, The Skull & Skibbereen, had a turntable and an engine shed at right angles to it. The same station had the main line approaching the platform at 90 degrees to it! Trains had to continue on to a spur and reverse round a curve to the station platform. Narrow-gauge railways are something of a law unto themselves, but I can't think of any other line where trains left a terminus travelling backwards!

CURVES

Curved sections of track are generally to a much larger radius on full-size railways, compared to scaled-down versions on model railways. A comparison that might give a feeling for this concerns the old tramway line to Weymouth harbour. This carried quite long trains, 'boat trains', which served the ships to the Channel Islands. The railway is an interesting survival, being largely intact – although trains haven't used it for some years.

At one time the railway had some particularly tight curves, so much so that to allow the corridor main-line coaches down to the harbour, special long-link couplings had to be fitted, instead of the coaches using screw-link couplings, which were the ones normally used. The gangway (corridor connections) between the coaches also needed to be disconnected. Only 0-6-0 locos would have been used on the Weymouth line at that time. The offending very sharpest curves were later eased by the Great Western Railway. Model main-line curves often scale down as sharper.

It is really surprising how modern model locos, with fewer visual compromises than their forebears, manage to negotiate these curves. In terms of model railways, it's always a matter of space where curves are concerned – not many modellers have the space for wide, sweeping curves. Since modern railway models and stock will negotiate fairly sharp curves, it is an idea to hide sharper curves in tunnels or have them disappear behind a backscene.

One frequent problem is storage on model railways – most don't have sufficient.

Transition curves can improve the appearance of curves, even on a layout formed of set track curves. Try using a sequence of set track pieces with a second radius piece in the middle, a third radius curve section on either side, then a fourth radius curve section following those.

If you want a circle with transition curves, another set of curves in the same sequence only reversed added on will create this. Of course, it is important to remember that the sharpest curve in the sequence will determine the minimum radius a train must be able to negotiate to be able to cope with it. This is known as the ruling radius of a curve.

MAIN-LINE STATIONS

Main-line stations are generally larger and more sophisticated versions of those found on secondary routes. Apart from the usual facilities for passengers, including buffets and kiosks selling newspapers, magazines and sweets, there would be offices, such as railway information offices. Some stations have overall roofs covering platforms and running lines.

Loco facilities would have been on a grander scale compared to what would be found on branch lines and modest cross-country lines. Turntables were often provided to turn locos. Sometimes the turntable would be situated in the centre of what was called a roundhouse, with sheds surrounding it. Where the only access to sheds was via a turntable, there was a problem if the turntable needed to be repaired and was therefore out of commission: the locos would effectively be marooned until the turntable came back into use. This situation can be exasperating on a model railway, too.

Facilities for diesel and electric locos and multiple unit stock were rather different to those relating to steam locomotives. Quite filthy conditions prevailed at steam sheds compared to diesel or electric motive power depots. Both types of shed situation make effective models, but the steam environment would need much more comprehensive weathering.

DRAWING UP LAYOUT PLANS

In my sketches of layouts I tend to represent points with two lines drawn at the angle to one another of the particular track system that it is intended to use. The drawn lines represent the centre lines of points and crossings. These simple outline drawings are to scale. It's easy to draw a sketch plan of a layout in this way.

Very fancy computer programs can be used to draw accurate track layout plans. These can be very good, but when evolving a basic layout plan, I personally enjoy the feedback between myself and a drawing, drawn up in the way I have described.

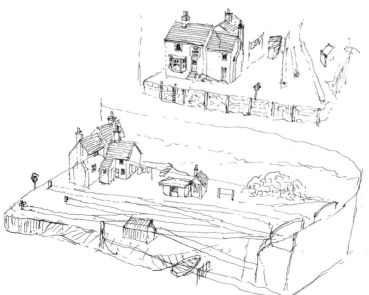

ABOVE: *Basic sketch of a model railway based on North Wales narrow-gauge lines – planning.*

LEFT: *Simple layout sketches for a 7mm scale layout – planning.*

Sketchbook page – planning.

Unfinished sketch of a possible layout in 0–16.5 7mm scale.

(continued overleaf)

(continued from previous page)

A completed layout based on Newton Abbot station. Only half the layout is shown. Built by Charles Benedetto and Brian Taylor.

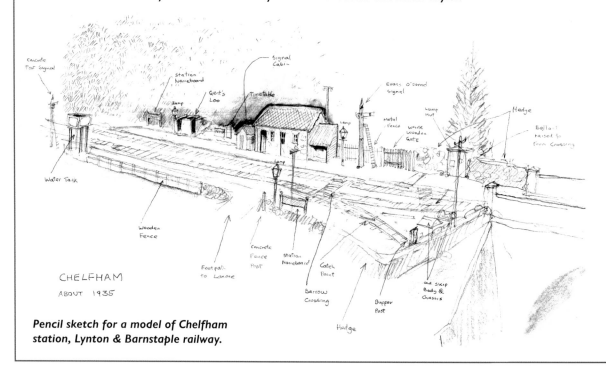

Pencil sketch for a model of Chelfham station, Lynton & Barnstaple railway.

I did a drawing of the wonderfully picturesque Salcombe Gullet (shame about the name!) in Devon, adding a railway bridge and embankment just to see if a railway would spoil the view.

I intended to make a model of this scene: 'The Narrows' in the Welshpool and Llanfair line. However, my half-timbered buildings ended up next to a road (Oxton).

WHERE TO PUT A MODEL RAILWAY

Finding a place to put a model railway is a problem these days. Traditionally, a place became available when the children left home, but these days they don't always leave because of the cost of buying or even renting a house.

In the past, modellers often based their layouts in sheds, but these tended to be freezing in winter and very hot in summer. Nowadays there are nice ranges of sheds available that are much more civilized, being fitted with insulation. However, an outside building has certain disadvantages: mains electricity is obviously needed; the building must be made secure; and insurance premiums are sometimes higher. Also, when strong sunlight shines through a window on to trackwork it can heat up and distort; it is therefore a good idea to have blinds. Equally, leaving tools in strong sunlight can give a nasty surprise to anyone picking them up. An indoor location for a railway layout obviously has the advantage of easier access to indoor facilities – besides which there is no trudging through inclement weather to reach the railway room – or trudging back to get to the toilet!

Cellars can be good places to install model railways, but they can be subject to damp (dehumidifiers are useful here), and sometimes height is restricted. If floors are uneven they will need to be levelled; and generally there is no natural light, although this might be seen as an advantage. Some people might find cellars claustrophobic, of course.

Another useful place for a model layout is a garage. Similar comments apply to garages as sheds, except where garages are connected to houses and access to them is through a door from the house. Where a garage has an up-and-over door, even if the garage is insulated and heated, the moment the door is opened, the heat will escape and the weather will come in! If you have definitely no intention to use the garage for

---

UNWANTED BENEVOLENCE

The concept of 'where to put a railway' reminds me of a story I was told of a modeller who built a G-scale layout in his garden. Once day he came home from work and found that his indoor 'N'-gauge layout had disappeared. He asked his wife about this and she said that since he had one railway he didn't need another in the house! She had given his layout to a charity shop.

Part of an 00/HO large layout built by Allen Etheridge and the author. Notice the RSJ – part of the roof structure of the house. The layout was placed very low to gain space.

RIGHT: *Part of the completed Swiss layout. The support tubes for the roof pass through the layout.*

BELOW: *A further view of the layout above, not quite completed.*

a car (many garages are too small for modern cars), a false wall can be built across the doorway with an outside domestic door. Mine was done with artificial shiplap boarding walling from a plastic window firm. The walling was fixed to a heavy wooden frame. If suitably treated and insulated, a garage then becomes a room.

CAUTIONARY TALES REGARDING LOFTS

A loft can be a good place for a layout. There are issues to consider, of course, such as height (some lofts are not high enough to stand up in) and the presence of structural members. Another factor is the size of the loft hatch; for instance, some can be quite small.

Lofts, like cellars, tend not to have windows, so will be unlikely to have natural lighting, though adding light is not difficult. Uninsulated loft spaces can suffer from temperature extremes, so installing insulation is a good idea.

A potential problem is that the joists in many roofs are not dimensioned to carry the weight of people, other than for occasional access to the loft space. Councils have regulations regarding the thickness of joists. It is a good idea to consult your council about any plans you might have, as they are usually helpful.

If you build a continuous layout in a loft, the slope of the roof will often reduce the possible width of the layout, the higher the baseboards are set. I was involved in building a layout where the roof had been reinforced by steel RSJs. To take maximum advantage of the space available the owner of the layout wanted it positioned as low as possible, though that meant getting close to the RSJs. It also meant that access under the layout was quite limited, and access was needed to reach the inside of certain tunnels. It turned out that the only person in the household able to do this was the wife of the layout owner – though I think she had mixed feelings about her new role!

Worthy of mention in this catalogue of hazards is a house fire that started quite close to a loft layout. The doorway leading to the loft storage area had a wooden lintel, but due to shortage of space a hole had been made in the chimney breast and the end of the lintel projected into the chimney! On this occasion the lintel end heated up to the point where it was smouldering, and set fire to a build-up of soot in the chimney. There was only one way up to the loft, which was via a staircase that went past the chimney breast and the end of the layout! Two fire engines were needed to put out the fire. Charles Benedetto and myself were in the loft working when this happened!

Loft layouts can be quite dangerous where access is through a hatch and this is left open. I once witnessed a very large old man narrowly escape a nasty fall. I also once met a modeller who had inherited his uncle's locomotives, having promised to build them a layout. A loft was chosen as the home for the layout. Before having this extensive loft layout, the nephew had spent most nights in a local bar with his friends. However,

his interest changed to running the railway with a few drinks thrown in. His friends soon joined him, and each evening was a bucolic affair, in the course of which the loft hatch was left open. It did occur to me that the mixture of trains, alcohol and an open loft hatch was likely to have only one outcome!

PORTABLE LAYOUTS

When deciding on a location for a layout, it is important to take into account whether a layout is going to be fixed and permanent, or portable, such as a layout that is frequently taken to exhibitions. With this in mind, a garage would be an excellent location if the layout is portable, with ground access and no stairs to carry the baseboards up and down. It is often awkward to carry layouts around corners, especially a series of corners in different directions!

Anyone who has staggered across an exhibition hall under the weight of a layout, or a section of one, will know that weight and size are big factors with model railways built for exhibitions, particularly if layout sections are moved on a regular basis. Furthermore, the weight of the boards is not the only factor to consider: there is also the weight of scenic elements. For example, if scenery on a layout includes rock faces cast in plaster, these will add appreciably to the weight of a board – likewise resin-cast buildings. Carrying a long heavy board any distance can be both awkward and exhausting.

If a layout is to be moved any distance, a long-wheelbase transit-type van will cope with a 2.4m (8ft) length of board, while a standard transit will take one of 2.1m (7ft) or so. These vehicles can be hired from firms specializing in van hire.

It is also important that the boards of portable layouts have convenient handholds so they can be held securely when they are being carried.

Where transportation is not a factor, there is something to be said for larger length boards up to 2.4m (8ft) long, if access problems – such as bends – don't prevent this. The longer the board, the fewer joints there will be, both electrical and structural. The width of a board must also be taken into account: in general, most people can reach across a 90cm (3ft)

SNAILSPEED 00 009

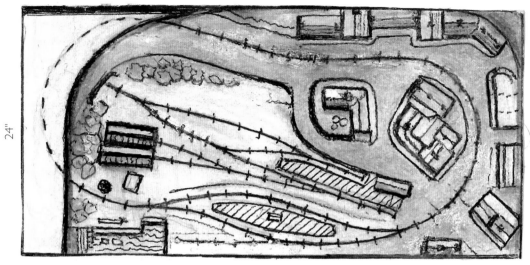

24"

51"

Snailspeed layout plan.

'Kit-bashed' station building.

THIS PAGE:
LEFT: Scratch- and kit-bashed buildings.

BELOW: Track 009 Peco – Peco code 100-00.

OPPOSITE PAGE:
TOP: Panorama of Snailspeed.

BOTTOM: The 'Prospect of Wimpy' pub, scratch built.

wide board if it is no more than 90cm above the ground. If in practice there will be easy access to both sides of the board, the possible width can be greater.

However, whether it is possible to use wider boards depends again on access. The width of a loft hatch can often restrict the possible width of boards.

CHAPTER FOUR

MAKING A BASEBOARD

There is no doubt that having a sound baseboard is a fundamental prerequisite for a model railway to run well. The question is – what makes an ideal baseboard? The answer used to be, in general, Sundeala board on a 2 × 1in softwood frame.

I once worked on a layout at Chapel-le-Ferne in Kent. This had lengths of supposedly straight track. It was immediately apparent that the track was not straight, so I re-set the track to line up with the edge of a long metal rule, then stood back and had a look. I was surprised to find that the track was still not straight, or didn't appear to be so. A closer look showed that the board was undulating up and down, due to damp.

The shed the layout was in was slightly damp, and the combination of this and too little bracing in the boards allowed this to happen. The board was Sundeala, which is a good baseboard, but it did require a lot of bracing. Trade manufacturers generally recommended Sundeala boards as a baseboard, and it was certainly good, but the reason the track makers

liked it was that it was easy to drive pins into it – in fact it was possible to push pins in without a hammer. Inexperienced modellers trying to drive pins into a harder board with a hammer, into the sleepers of potentially delicate trackwork, were bound to struggle – and faced with an apparently 'unyielding' material, might even damage the trackwork.

For a long time my favourite baseboard material was MDF, but later I became converted to plywood, having worked on a layout in a very damp garage. We had to assemble the layout after the boards had been stored in these extremely damp surroundings for years. The boards came together easily and seemed surprisingly little affected by their long sojourn in the garage. This example of long-term durability under difficult conditions was impressive, and I have tended to use birch ply all but exclusively since. It is advisable to have the boards professionally cut.

It is probably best to get the boards cut to size by the woodyard that supplied them. Starting assembly

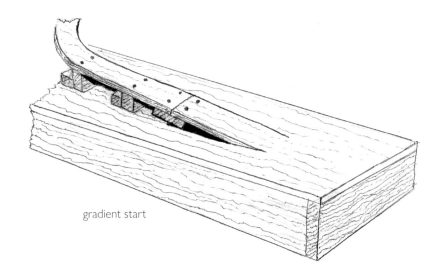

gradient start

Making a gradient.

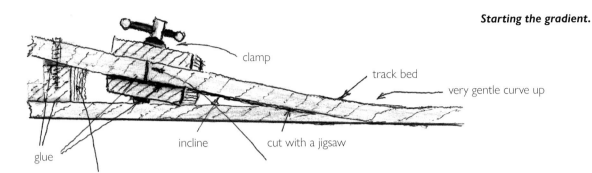

Starting the gradient.

clamp

track bed

very gentle curve up

incline

cut with a jigsaw

glue

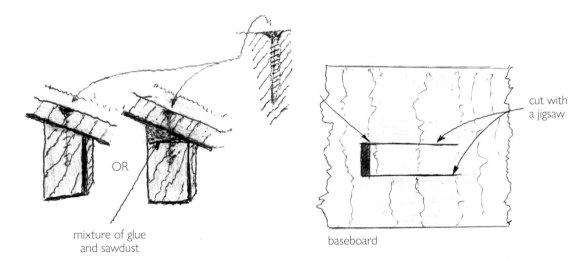

OR

mixture of glue
and sawdust

cut with
a jigsaw

baseboard

Supporting a gradient.

Making the first cuts at the start of a gradient.

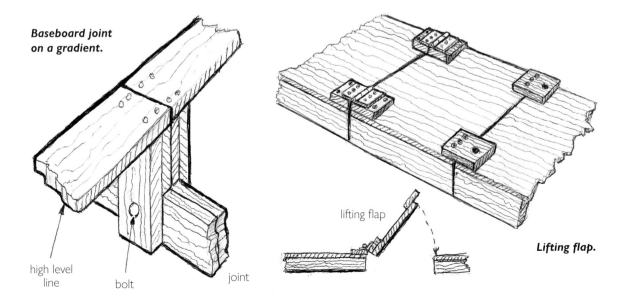

*Baseboard joint
on a gradient.*

high level
line

bolt

joint

lifting flap

Lifting flap.

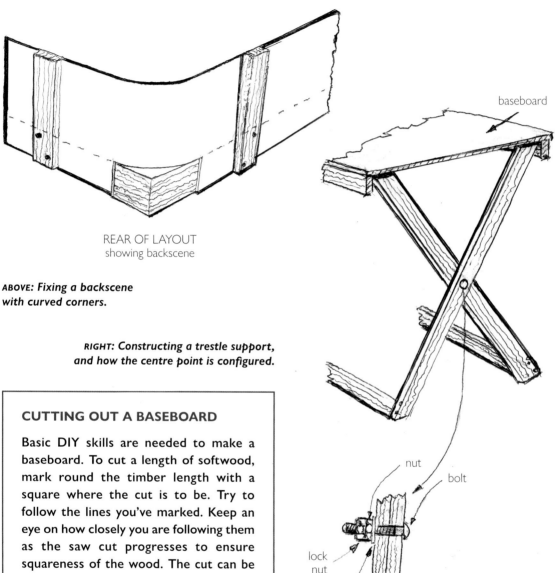

REAR OF LAYOUT
showing backscene

*ABOVE: Fixing a backscene
with curved corners.*

*RIGHT: Constructing a trestle support,
and how the centre point is configured.*

baseboard

nut

bolt

lock
nut

washer

CUTTING OUT A BASEBOARD

Basic DIY skills are needed to make a baseboard. To cut a length of softwood, mark round the timber length with a square where the cut is to be. Try to follow the lines you've marked. Keep an eye on how closely you are following them as the saw cut progresses to ensure squareness of the wood. The cut can be done with a small general-purpose saw or a tenon saw. Larger saws with bigger teeth are needed to cut along the grain, as opposed to making cross cuts; these saws are known as rip saws. For making cross cuts a small circular saw can also be used. An electric jigsaw is useful for cutting out curves, especially the flat sheets of ply for baseboard tops. They can also be used for cross-cutting timber lengths. Finer blades avoid 'tearing' the surface.

of layout boards with them already cut to shape accurately means that it is possible to start work on the bracing immediately. I have generally used 3 × 1in softwood for this, while 6mm ply is the usual thickness chosen for the baseboard itself. When gradients are added this is easily done by cutting the track bed with a jigsaw, and gently forming the start of the bed to flow from the main board (see diagram).

Ideally make up boards on a flat floor – probably the most likely place is a garage floor. The best size for individual boards is the largest practical. There will be fewer joints between boards because fewer boards will be necessary. There will also be fewer electrical connections, of course. If the boards need to be portable, size will be a problem. Negotiating stairs can be tricky, especially if bends are involved. If a layout is to be situated in a loft and there is a loft hatch, the size of this will need to be taken into account.

CONSTRUCTING THE FRAME

A very solid and simple way of constructing a baseboard is to add the lengths of softwood one by one. These lengths are not usually very straight, and the best way of fitting them is by pinning them down, making sure with each pin that they are in line with the edge of the boards. You will probably find that the frame timbers will need pushing back in line with the baseboard as you pin them to the boards. It is better not to glue the softwood to ply (or whatever surface material is used) since the pine and board will not expand and contract at the same rate – if they are firmly fixed together, pinning alone will allow enough 'give' to stop the baseboard from 'twisting'.

A convenient way of creating legs is simply to use lengths of 2 × 2in softwood, which can be fixed neatly inside the joints between the lengths of 3 × 1in. The greater depth of the frame is useful here. This would not be so satisfactory with 2 × 1in as a framing material.

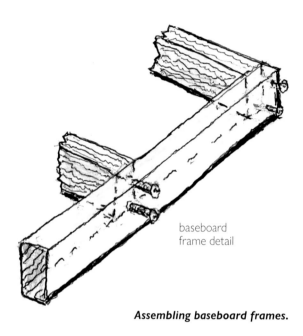

baseboard frame detail

Assembling baseboard frames.

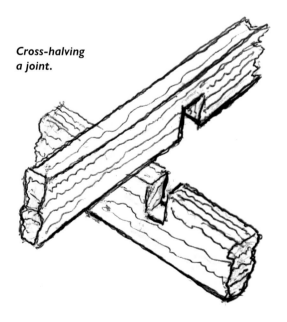

Cross-halving a joint.

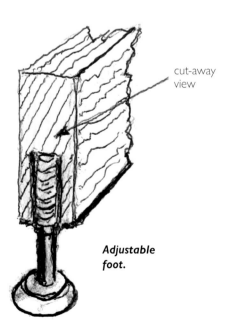

cut-away view

Adjustable foot.

Fitting legs.

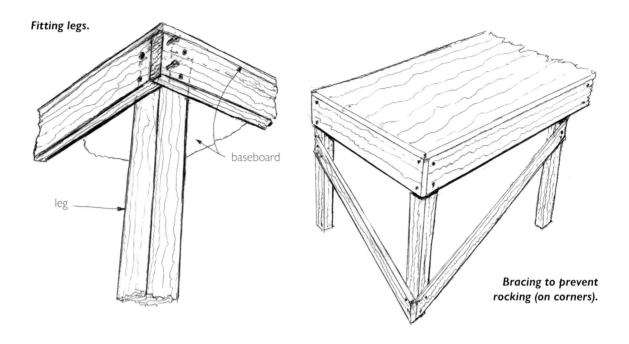

leg

baseboard

Bracing to prevent rocking (on corners).

OXTON 0–16.5

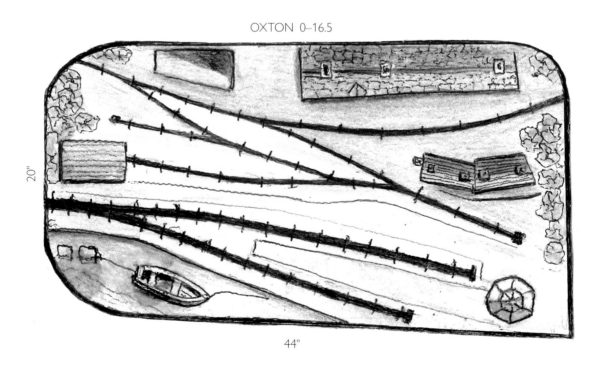

20"

44"

ABOVE: Oxton layout plan.

OPPOSITE PAGE:
TOP: Looking down the street – card sheet.

BOTTOM: Building card Peco Glyn Valley tram loco kit.

OPPOSITE PAGE:
TOP: Scratch-built shelter, cast seat figures.

BOTTOM: Scratch-built card buildings. Newhaven West Quay, beacon.

THIS PAGE:
RIGHT: 'Brighton Terrier' loco.

BELOW: Main street.

FITTING CROSS BATTENS

When it comes to fitting battens to support the middle areas of a board, some modellers wait until the track is laid and the position of any points is known. This avoids fitting battens where point motors should be placed. Finding this out after battens are fitted is very frustrating! Where boards such as Sundeala are used, these will need more bracing, so cross battens are more likely to be in the way of point motors, if the battens are put in before fitting them.

CHAPTER FIVE

SET TRACKS, BASIC TRACK LAYING AND FLEXIBLE TRACK

SECTIONAL TRACK

Since the early days of model railways, a layout started with some kind of flat surface and a collection of track pieces that could be pushed together. Often at the end of a running session the lengths of track were gently pulled apart and placed in a box ready for the next running session. When I was a child, these occasions where a train ran took place on the floor. My father often mentioned getting a board on which to set up the track, but this didn't happen, and eventually I set up my track on a worktop in my bedroom. These worktops were actually intended as places where I could sit and do my homework!

The sectional tracks available then were beefier than they are now. The rails had a larger section and were intended for a hard life. Modern sectional track systems are not so solidly made in comparison, but look more realistic than when I was a child. In addition to Triang tracks, which were two rail, there were two three-rail systems, one made by Hornby, the other by Trix.

Currently the only mainstream system available that has electrical pickup in the centre of the track is Märklin; available for many years, it does not have a centre rail but has a series of studs electrically connected to one another instead. The system works well, and the studs are not obtrusive.

There are two types of sectional track: the first has a base that includes moulded ballast. The second type of track does not have this, and the moulded bases purely represent sleepers. In general, where moulded ballast is provided this is not very realistic, though weathering can help.

Deciding which of these track systems is the best is largely down to personal preference. Inevitably some tracks will be judged to look 'toy train set' more than others – though to many people this is not an issue. What is most important is reliability over a long term. Of course, if the track pieces are put together and taken apart on a frequent basis their working life might be shorter than if the tracks are assembled together and then kept in place. Care when putting lengths of sectional track together will also increase the life of the track pieces.

Where track bases just represent sleepers, any ballasting is up to the modeller, and this generally leads to a more realistic effect. Of course, model railways are such a broad church, and expectations of them are very diverse. A fine scale modeller who makes his own track to dimensions very close to scaled-down versions of the real thing will see most other track systems as

---

FUN WITH A SIMPLE SET-TRACK CIRCLE

It is surprising how a simple circle of set track with a train running on it can fascinate people. An exhibition designer friend decided to have a model railway in the entrance to an exhibition stand to draw the public in. The stand was for an oil company and the train of tankers were lettered with the company name. This exhibit proved such a success that it had to be moved as onlookers blocked the entrance.

being very toy like, whereas someone who wants to just watch trains chase their tails round a very basic continuous layout would be astonished by the lengths some modellers go to achieve the ultimate in scale accuracy. Nobody is right or wrong here, there is just a difference of priorities. Since model railways are a hobby for most people, the important thing is that everyone finds the hobby satisfying and enjoyable. It can be challenging, too, but that is not to everyone's taste.

So for many people, plastic-based track systems with ballast moulded in are ideal forms of track because with a minimum of fuss and bother they can have neat-looking trackwork on which trains will run well and reliably. The fact that the tracks will not be the last word in prototypical exactitude isn't an issue for many people.

SECTIONAL TRACK WITHOUT BALLAST

With this type of sectional track the modeller must ballast the track himself. One advantage of some types of section track is their compatibility with certain types of flexible track. I'll cover this in some detail later in the book. With these various types of sectional track, it is still important to lay them as well as possible on a flat surface. One apparent advantage of these tracks is the apparent speed with which they can be laid. However, it is necessary to take care over the process and fit the sections together carefully. Things to watch are the following:

- Lay the track carefully – don't force the rails together.
- Be careful not to push the rails into the fishplates and find that, rather than sliding properly in place, the fishplates have been pushed under the rails.
- Sectional tracks are usually available in several different radii. If you are laying a circle of track be careful to use curves of the same radius, otherwise when you push the rail sections together gaps will be apparent on one side. This can happen anyway, with careless assembly.
- If the track is to be taken apart after a running session it is not a good idea to 'waggle' the tracks to separate them. This causes the fishplates to open

HISTORICAL – NEW TRACKS FOR OLD

Some time ago I was involved in the construction of a model rail that was to be the home of a large collection of pre-war Hornby 3-rail '0' equipment. We used replica Hornby track which is commercially available. This track system featured points of rather larger radius than the original Hornby track work. The gentler curves were used, with deference to the age of the locos and stock.

When the original Hornby collection was united with the new layout it became apparent that the collection contained a great many original Hornby scenic details and buildings, all of which were in a charming 1930s style. In comparison with modern model railways the locos and stock are seriously compromised in scale terms, and yet there is a delightful feel to everything, a sense of design. Many items are tin plate, and the printing was particularly colourful. In some respects, the overall look is of an attractive caricature of a railway. The type of sectional track described above is also suitable for modern locos based on coarse scale '0'-gauge standards.

up, making a looser fit and poorer electrical contacts – this also goes for putting the tracks together.
- It is also important not to bend the rails of the fishplates in the vertical plane.
- Try to avoid track joints coinciding with baseboard joints.

When track is fixed down to some form of baseboard the questions are first, how to fix it – that is, by pinning or gluing; and whether to use some form of underlay between the track and the baseboard.

VIBRATION AND BALLASTING

If you connect a model railway loco motor to a controller, when the motor is running it will produce a noise. This is due to vibration of the motor, inducing audible soundwaves in the air. If you hold the motor against a baseboard when it is running, the sound will be much louder and deeper. A loco with a similar motor running on a track on the board will produce a similar sound. The baseboard will in fact be behaving like a 'sounding board'. An example of a sounding board is to be found on a piano.

If a motor, instead of being held against the board, is held against a piece of foam rubber that is fixed to the board, to some extent the motor will be 'de-coupled' acoustically from the board by the foam. Depending on the particular properties of the foam, sound transmitted through the foam from the motor to the board may well be less with the foam in place.

A number of manufacturers make foam underlays for track. Over the years I've come across layouts using foam underlay where the foam has disintegrated, becoming a powder, or a sticky mess, or both. The question is, do modern foam materials disintegrate in the same fashion? The answer from the manufacturers is always in the negative, of course. The foam underlays don't deaden the sound, rather they prevent the vibration to some extent from the loco and the train passing from the track to the baseboard.

The subject of vibration is a complex one. A favourite material to place between track and baseboard is cork. If track is ballasted and the cork is saturated with dilute PVA adhesive to take a layer of ballast, when this dries the cork can become rock hard and useful qualities of the cork are lost – other than raising the track bed.

With materials such as cork, the difference between pinning and gluing down the track is interesting. Securely pinning down the track with a cork base, for example, causes the vibrations from the track to reach the baseboard through the track pins. Gluing down the track enables it to some extent to float on the cork. It is also quite hard to pin down track on a cork base without ending up with the pins pushing the sleeper tops a little way into the cork and creating an undulating track bed rather than a flat one.

One way round this is to not completely pin down the track but leave it floating with the pin heads a small distance from the sleeper tops. People often talk of sound deadening, but this is quite difficult to achieve, as it involves damping due to the internal friction of a material, when unwanted energy is converted into heat and lost. Where attempts are made to reduce audible sound from baseboards by stiffening them up by adding bracing, this often just pushes up the frequency of the sound, without reducing its intensity much.

BALLASTING BASEBOARDS

If you hold up a piece of board and tap it, you will hear the natural resonant frequency of the board. If you brace the board, that frequency will be higher. If you run a train on a board and the resonant frequency of the train coincides with that of the board, the sound intensity will be highest. Foam underlay is quite effective as a means of keeping vibrations from trains causing baseboards to vibrate, but appearance is not particularly realistic, and painting these lengths of foam tends to stiffen up the material and change its vibrational characteristics. Pinning the track down with these materials also tends to transmit the track vibrations to the main baseboard, and so rather defeats the object of using the foam.

Layouts are often ballasted with fine granite chips glued in place with thinned PVA adhesive with a dash of washing-up liquid to overcome the surface tension of the dilute glue. This looks good, but creates a rock-hard permanent way very solidly attached to the baseboard. It is fairly easy to see that creating a noiseless vibrational free layout is not easy to achieve, especially bearing in mind the many compromises involved in building a model railway. Unwanted noise is more of a factor than it used to be because of the presence of realistic simulated sounds onboard model locos and trains fitted with suitable electronics.

BASIC TRACK LAYING
LEVELLING THE BASEBOARD
Before laying track it is important that the baseboard is level. Level is one of those awkward words that have more than one meaning. Level can mean flat, but it can

PRACTICAL EXPERIENCE WITH VIBRATION

For many years I was involved in building model railways in a bespoke manner for people. Usually we used 6mm birch ply for baseboards, framed with 3 × 1in prepared softwood framing, with legs of 2 × 2in prepared softwood. Track was mostly Peco, ballasted with granite ballast. The track was generally pinned down directly to the boards.

This method of construction proved very durable and trouble free over the years – the oldest layouts were built twenty-five years ago or more. Where a particularly acoustically 'dead' baseboard was needed we added a layer of fibreboard to the plywood main board to further reduce the noise thresholds. Noise didn't normally present a problem with these construction techniques. But it is important to add that in some rooms the acoustic behaviour of the room can exaggerate noise due to a layout.

Vibration is not just a problem in terms of audible noise. For example, where vibrations pass from a train to the track a 'chattering' effect can be created between the track and train. This can be caused by energy being passed backwards and forwards between the two, and can cause the wheels to lose contact momentarily with the track due to vibration. Current pick-up between the train and the track is then interrupted, and adds to the effects of dirt on the rails in terms of current collection loss; it can also affect train adhesion.

When vibration reaches the baseboard, its audible effect will be noticeable. Stiffening up a board by adding bracing will tend to push up the overall resonant frequency, usually without a noticeable reduction in its sound level. If the resonant frequency coincides with the band of frequencies at which the ear is most sensitive, its audible effect will be potentially most annoying and subsequently most obtrusive. To some extent, it comes down to a matter of opinion as to which frequency is most acceptable that a baseboard 'sings' at!

If you can keep the train vibration away from the baseboard itself by some form of de-coupling – for example, a layer of foam between the sleepers and the board – that may well be the best course. However, beware! If you fix point motors to the more solid baseboard beneath the foam, rather than to the foam, with the operating pin of the solenoid motor passing through the layers of boards to the tie-bar of the motor, vibrations will pass through the pin to the main baseboard. The same goes for anything that can potentially connect to the main baseboard.

also mean the type you can measure with a spirit level. A glass of water shows the same thing if you look at the water level. When you look at the reading on a spirit level sitting on a baseboard, which is supposed to be parallel with the floor, the spirit level will probably show that it is not level.

If you build a baseboard that is supposed to be parallel with a floor that isn't level in absolute terms, lay a length of track and sit a wagon on it, and the wagon will run downhill (in the direction the floor slopes). So if you want wagons to stay where they are in a siding

and not run off down the line, if not connected to a loco, the track should be spirit-level level. This can be most easily accomplished with the help of adjustable feet or just padding under the baseboards.

The other level relates to the flatness of a surface. To accomplish this the following are useful:

● A band of sandpaper that can be slid round a block of wood – usually provided by the customer. It is fairly important to use the right size block. Too slack and the band of abrasive will keep coming off; too tight and it will be hard to fit in the first place. A number of different abrasive strength bands are available. Little skill is needed to use these blocks. There are a number of different types of abrasive blocks available.

- Various tools are also available. However, a plane is probably the most effective, in spite of it being one of the oldest tools, in terms of its use dating back to ancient times.
- Electric sanders can be used to flatten trackbeds, but with these it is easy to take off too much.

Whether we are talking about sectional or flexible track, the basic rules are the same.

LAYING DOWN THE TRACK

Once the basic trackbed is flat we can consider laying down the track; there are a number of ways of doing this.

Pinning down is probably the most popular way of laying tracks. Various pins are available that are suitable for pinning down track. The most commonly used on a layout is probably the flat-headed pin, which looks like a small conventional nail. These can be driven into baseboards with a suitable hammer, though how easily this can be done depends on the hardness of the baseboard. A pilot hole can be drilled to make driving in the pin somewhat easier. The best way of determining the pilot hole size – which obviously needs to be smaller than the pin shank size – is to select a drill size, drive a pin into the board, and try it. Section track often has holes in the sleepers for pinning, whereas flexible track systems don't so much.

The bane of track laying is bending track pins, and probably causes more bad language than any other task in railway modelling! This is particularly so with the very thin pins that were originally intended for Sundeala board and other soft boards, into which pins can be pushed easily. With other boards it is rather different, as these pins bend very easily. The task is made easier with curved pliers, which grip the pins easily; these pliers are thin, or snipe nosed. It is relatively quite easy to hold the pins with these and tap them in gently through the sleepers and into the board. A pilot hole is still probably worthwhile.

In terms of visibility, I suppose the 'thin pin' type of pin, with its small head, should be less obvious visually than the flat-headed type, as the head is very thin and not that easy to see when in place. What makes it more noticeable is the slightly different sheen and sometimes colour of some sleepers. So provided that the track is weathered, the appearance of the flat-head pins is fine. I would certainly recommend that less experienced modellers use the flat-head type. (Weathering track will be covered later.)

If you have already pinned down some track and aren't satisfied with it, a good tool to lift the track without damaging it is to slide a thin scraper under it and gently ease it up. If the track is ballasted the glue bond can be released by pouring hot water on the track. How easily the track can be lifted depends to some extent on the strength of the adhesive itself. For example, three parts water to one part PVA and a little washing-up liquid is a common ratio.

THE SPACING BETWEEN TRACKS

Another consideration with track laying is the spacing between the tracks. Usually with commercial trackwork this distance between the rails is exaggerated compared to that of a prototype railway. This is because the overhang of coaches on curves risks them hitting oncoming coaches on the other line. The tighter the curves, the greater the distance needs to be. Station platforms should also be made with this in mind to avoid vehicles hitting the platform sides.

Set-track curves are designed to have a distance apart to alleviate clearance problems on curves. Small plastic gauges are available to check this from firms such as Peco. Where set-track points are concerned when set as crossovers the distance between the inside rail and outside rail when used with radius 2 and radius 3 curves is enough for clearance between most vehicles likely to be run.

LAYING FLEXIBLE TRACK

I remember when Peco flexible track appeared, and for the first time transition curves became possible without scratch building track formations. Trackwork could be made to seem flowing, with very little

ABOVE: Set-track curves can be used with compatible flexible track systems with more sophisticated pointwork – for example Peco set track and streamline points. Here, first-radius set curves have been used with large-radius turnouts (points) to give an effect of transition curves.

RIGHT: The other side of the layout. The narrow gauge was a later addition.

effort. Using flexible track and associated pointwork, with its more authentic-looking geometry, it is quite straightforward to make fairly life-like examples of model permanent way.

Like any ready-to-run track, care is needed, and we will look at the 'wrinkles' in laying flexible track, and how with the code 100 track, set-track curves can be used to produce authentic-looking trackwork in surprisingly small spaces. Where space is available, apparently sweeping curves can be employed without recourse to visual illusion.

MAKING JOINTS ON CURVES

Much of what I have written about set tracks applies to flexible track. The obvious difference is that curves will not stay where they are put without being fixed down. Making joints on curves is difficult if the track is butt jointed, as the tracks try and spring out of alignment. I tend to splice the tracks together. This is accomplished by taking two lengths of track and cutting one rail back on alternate sides; the longer length of rail, not cut, can slide into the rail fixings left empty on the other piece of the track, and vice versa. This gives a staggered joint and allows the track to flow more easily. The fishplates on the shortened rails can be fitted by trimming the rail fixings. Although rather fiddly, this is a fairly foolproof way of creating a good joint on a curve.

Where fishplates are to be fitted, the rail fixings need to be trimmed back. It is possible to push fishplates through the rail fixing so they don't need to be cut, but there is a knack to doing this and less experienced modellers should cut the rail fixings!

There are various methods of cutting the rails. A fine-toothed razor saw can be used; mini-drills with cutting discs are an alternative and mechanized way of cutting track; and track cutters are another method. I tend to use track cutters such as Xuron cutters, and file back the rail heads appropriately. A useful simple kit of tools would be a track-cutting device of choice, a hammer, a knife (I use a scalpel) for trimming rail fixings, webs and so on, also a soldering iron, solder and various files. A pin vice is also useful, and small drills for pilot holes for pins.

MORE TRACK-LAYING HINTS

I have talked about 'servicing hammers', and because hammers do collect grease on their heads, it is a good idea to rub the heads with emery paper to clean them. This treatment helps stop hammer heads sliding off pins when they are being hit, which can be annoying!

Sometimes it is easier to put in two points or more, and then add the plain track between them afterwards.

The layout shown was built with a circle of second-radius set track buried in green flock. The scale is 0-16.5.

An earlier view of a layout that attempts to use a set track in a similar manner; it shows what happens if you don't quite cover the sleepers 0-16.5. The track in the distance is Lima '0'-gauge sectional track.

The Lima track again, which doesn't look out of place on a light railway, as the rails are of quite fine section. The same rails were used on Lima HO-gauge track. The layout was built by the late Maggie Pettett and the author – Pagglesham.

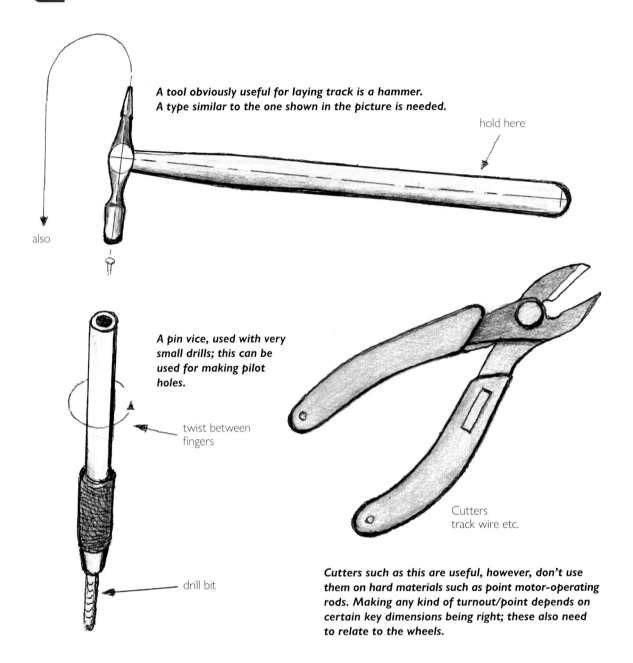

A tool obviously useful for laying track is a hammer. A type similar to the one shown in the picture is needed.

hold here

also

A pin vice, used with very small drills; this can be used for making pilot holes.

twist between fingers

drill bit

Cutters
track wire etc.

Cutters such as this are useful, however, don't use them on hard materials such as point motor-operating rods. Making any kind of turnout/point depends on certain key dimensions being right; these also need to relate to the wheels.

The wider radius points/turnouts that match the flexible track can be laid in the same manner as the set-track points. However, the set-track points/turnouts have pin holes right through the sleepers, whereas, for example, Peco Streamline points have holes only part of the way through, which need drilling out for pins. (Of course, if the track is being glued down, this won't be necessary.)

STICKING TRACK DOWN

Gluing track down is a perfectly acceptable way of installing it. Once the adhesive has dried, strategically placed pins can be added for extra strength. N-gauge flexible track is somewhat more fiddly to lay than that of the larger scales, because the sleepers are very narrow and drilling them to take pins is quite awkward. The track, can be glued, which obviates this problem.

Peco fine-scale track in N is rather peculiar to lay. Like flexible track in general, fine-scale N track has ties missing between some of the sleepers, to allow the track to flex without buckling. Peco might have changed this since I last used it, but fine-scale N track has more ties missing on one side compared to the other. This means that the track curves to a tighter radius one way compared to the other.

By very clever design, although the rail section looks lighter than the standard 'N'-gauge rail, which is code 80, parts of the rail sections are buried in the sleepers – code 55 track without it being flimsy and delicate to handle!

FLEXIBLE TRACK WITH SET TRACK

Various elements of the code 100 flexible-track systems can be used with set track where there have to be very sharp curves. Set-track curves are best used, being machine made and therefore accurate to gauge and radius, since laying flexible track to these standards is difficult. According to Peco, the various radii of set-track curves in '00' gauge are:

- First radius: 371mm (14⅝in)
- Second radius: 438mm (17¼in)
- Third radius: 505mm (19⅞in)
- Fourth radius: 571.5mm (22½in)

Some commercial ready-to-run vehicles will not traverse first radius (14⅝in) curves, though most will traverse second radius (17¼in). It is quite possible to use second radius.

TRANSITION SET TRACK

For a minimum radius on a small continuous layout but linking the set-track curves to larger radius Streamline points, the larger radii can give the look of a transition curve in conjunction with the set-track curves. Trains not passing from straight track directly into a very sharp curve will look more realistic. On a small layout I had, there was a series of Streamline larger radius points/turnouts followed by 17¼ radius second-radius set track, followed by a tunnel. At a show someone

remarked about the sharp curve. I asked him what he guessed the radius was, and he said, 'about 30in'. He was quite surprised when I said it was only 17¼. Of course, 30in is still a sharp curve in real terms, but the overall visual effect of the layout was surprisingly spacious for its size.

Surprising things are possible from this approach.

GLUING TECHNIQUE

If you decide to glue down flexible track, a good technique seems to be to apply UHU or a Bostic type of adhesive to a piece of thin card, and wipe it over the base of some track. Be sparing with this. Do a short section of track and stick it down. You will be able to move the track for a while before the glue goes off. The rest of the length of the track can be treated in the same way, but the piece of card with the adhesive can be slid underneath the track. The track can be moved about a little until it is aligned correctly, then it can be pressed down using finger pressure.

MORE TRACK-LAYING HINTS

Pins can be added if desired. To lift the track prior to any pins being put in, a thin scraper can be slid under the track. This can be done even after the glue has gone off. If there are any places where the glue is not holding the track, slide a piece of card, perhaps thinner than the first one, under the track. Then again, press down with finger pressure. Should the original glue have gone hard and a thickness prevents the track being pushed down flat, push the scraper backwards and forwards to remove the glue, then vacuum off the residue.

If it is felt that templates would be useful when laying the track, these can be made from 2mm card (mounting card is available from art shops and stationers). The templates can be lightly pinned, and the inner rail of the track pushed up against the template. The track can be either pinned or glued down, then the template can be removed.

I mentioned earlier that a useful track-laying ploy is to use set track and flexible track together. A point I should mention is that if you need to remove the fishplates on set track the plates are spot welded to the rails. They aren't hard to remove: just grip the

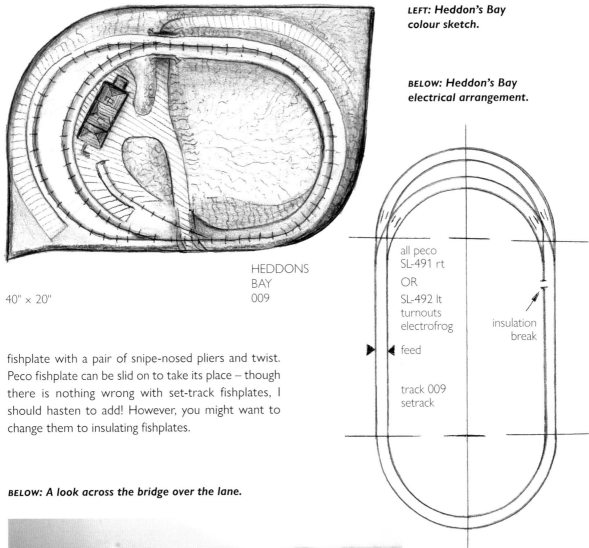

LEFT: Heddon's Bay colour sketch.

BELOW: Heddon's Bay electrical arrangement.

HEDDONS
BAY
009

40" × 20"

all peco
SL-491 rt
OR
SL-492 lt
turnouts
electrofrog

feed

track 009
setrack

insulation
break

fishplate with a pair of snipe-nosed pliers and twist. Peco fishplate can be slid on to take its place – though there is nothing wrong with set-track fishplates, I should hasten to add! However, you might want to change them to insulating fishplates.

BELOW: A look across the bridge over the lane.

OPPOSITE PAGE:
TOP: Station view looking across country.

BOTTOM: Station building.

Past the station down the layout.

View across the layout; the twin hills exist in reality and are known as 'Great and Little Hangmen' (backscene).

FAME FOR A SMALL RAILWAY WHEN IT CLOSED

The day before the Lynton and Barnstaple Railway closed in 1935 a cameraman from *The Times* arrived in North Devon to take photos for the newspaper. A chosen shot was of a train high on the hillside just outside Lynton. The photo turned out to be stunning, even though it was in black and white – so I decided to have a go at translating the picture into a colour portrait. Recently I thought I might make a diorama based on the scene, a sort of working *Times* photo! I was quite pleased with the result: a little train, high on the hillside above the East Lyn valley, against the background of the Devon hills with Exmoor visible in the distance – though I didn't manage to restage exactly the scene of the photo, because the hillside always got in the way! One of the photos is reproduced here, together with my painted version of *The Times* picture, taken in 1935 for comparison.

ABOVE: *The author's version of* **The Times** *photograph in colour. Painted in gouache with watercolour pencil.*

LEFT: *Model – Helgian OO9 L&B loco (with pony wheels removed for freedom on OO9 set-track curves), and Peco Lynton & Barnstaple Railway coaches on the hillside.*

CHAPTER SIX

KEEPING ON THE RIGHT TRACK, AND RAILS AND TRAIN WEIGHTS

Trains are more likely to come off rails passing through a point than anywhere else.

Unlike a plain crossing, where one set of lines crosses another, a point has the added complication of moving parts – point blades (switch tongues).

KEEPING ON THE TRACK

VITAL DIMENSIONS

There are some very important dimensions, you could call these vital statistics, which if they are not right, cause derailments or give vehicles a very bumpy ride through a point/crossing. One crucial consideration regarding points and crossings is that a vehicle won't take a 'wrong turn' at a crossing – trying to travel down the wrong line or simply hitting the crossing nose.

Check Rails

Because wheel sets consist of two wheels solidly fixed to an axle, if you restrict the sideways movement of one wheel, the other wheel will be forced to follow suit. So, placing a short length of rail (check rail) alongside the main running rail, opposite the crossing nose (frog), stops the inside wheel of a set from drifting across and running 'wrong road' through a crossing, or hitting the crossing nose – which would almost certainly cause a derailment.

Wing Rails

Either side of the crossing nose is a rail known as a wing rail. If the distance between the back of one wheel in a wheel set to the back of another is smaller than a certain distance, the wheels will jam against the

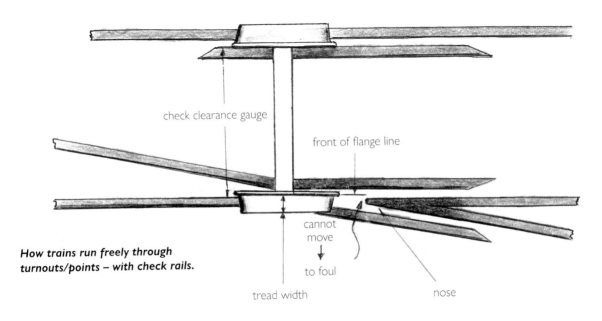

check clearance gauge

front of flange line

cannot
move
↓
to foul

tread width

nose

How trains run freely through turnouts/points – with check rails.

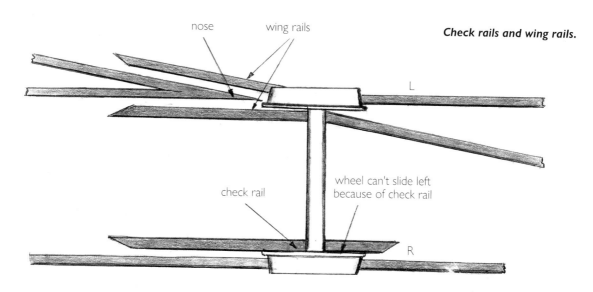

Check rails and wing rails.

check rail on one side, and on the other, one of the wing rails. If the wheels are set too far apart a wheel might derail, riding up the crossing nose. Track and wheel standards should be compatible.

'Back-to-Back' Gauge

The distance between the backs of the two wheels and the flanges to one another is called the 'back-to-back' gauge and is clearly an important measurement, though what is known as the 'front-to-back' gauge (the distances between the back of one wheel and the

front of the flange of the other) is considered more meaningful, as it allows for wheel flange thickness.

Widening flangeway width and increasing tyre widths on vehicle wheels can result in dimensions being less critical. But wheels tend to drop into the wider crossing gaps with a somewhat unrealistic 'bump'.

Maintaining Clearances

Some track systems over the years have been described as universal – capable of accommodating 'fine scale' or 'coarse scale' wheels. The old Peco universal track

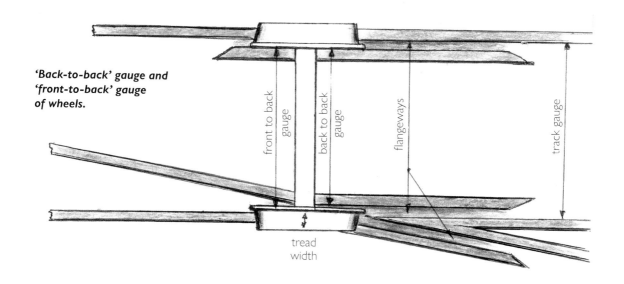

'Back-to-back' gauge and 'front-to-back' gauge of wheels.

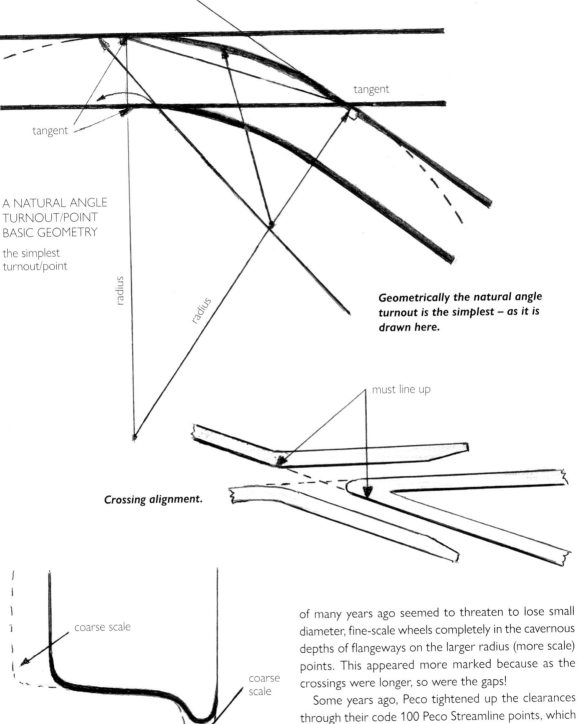

A NATURAL ANGLE TURNOUT/POINT BASIC GEOMETRY

the simplest turnout/point

tangent

tangent

radius

radius

Geometrically the natural angle turnout is the simplest – as it is drawn here.

must line up

Crossing alignment.

coarse scale

coarse scale

Rough sketch showing fine- and coarse-scale wheel profiles.

of many years ago seemed to threaten to lose small diameter, fine-scale wheels completely in the cavernous depths of flangeways on the larger radius (more scale) points. This appeared more marked because as the crossings were longer, so were the gaps!

Some years ago, Peco tightened up the clearances through their code 100 Peco Streamline points, which gave for better running. This was possible due to modern commercial wheels being noticeably finer than their predecessors of some years ago. Peco also produced a range of trackwork in code 75 rail. Most

Wing rails.

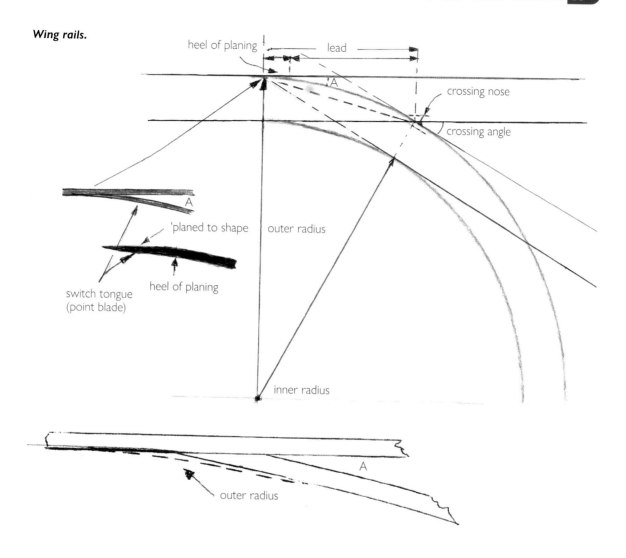

modern commercial stock will negotiate this – Peco fine-scale track. Of course, Peco also produce bullhead track, which suits steam-era layouts and early diesel lines well. There is a good deal of real bullhead track still about – for example, as sidings for permanent way vehicles and stores – and not forgetting there is plenty of bullhead track to be seen as preserved railways.

BULLHEAD TRACKS

The rails on bullhead track are supported on cast chairs, which act as seats for the rails and grasp them in conjunction with spring keys. Bullhead pointwork involved quite a few special chairs. Chairs have often been portrayed using solder blobs on printed circuit-

board sleepers. The blobs also hold the rails in place. Real cast chairs have a detailed, complex appearance, which of course is only superficially 'blob' like.

Sometimes bullhead-railed flexible track is used with printed circuit-board sleepered points of soldered (blob) construction, when the detailed appearance of the moulded plastic plain track will tend to draw attention to the lack of detail of soldered pointwork. When track is soldered throughout, the overall visual effect quite often looks better because of the consistency of the appearance of all the track. Sometimes when comparisons are directly possible, such as in this, shortcomings can be shown up that otherwise would perhaps not be noticeable.

LOOKING AGAIN AT POINTS/TURNOUTS

What does a point/turnout consist of? All trackwork is made from basic units. The first is a common crossing – so called because there are many of them around and they allow one line to cross another. A turnout also has switch(es) or point blades (model railway language), which are machined to fit against what are known as the stock rails. Which way the blades/switches are set determines the route that is taken by a train.

The smoothness of the passage of a train through a crossing depends on the alignment of the rails, and the track standards (measurements) being compatible with wheel standards, which relate to the various dimensions of a wheel set, as we have seen earlier.

Various gauges are available, which help set up the clearances of model railway pointwork. These of course are only needed if points are assembled by hand. Ready-to-run points come already set up in this regard. But wheel standards still need to be compatible with those of the track.

I have included a diagram showing the various parts of a typical point/turnout. All the various items of trackwork, however complex, contain the elements in the conventional point/turnout. The principal types of pointwork are described below.

STANDARD POINTS

In a standard point/turnout there is what is known as a straight road and a diverging road. The diverging road track 'turns out' from the straight road, and can be either left- or right-handed (a basic description of turnout/point curves practice is to be found in the first chapter of this book). Point curves can be plain radius curves, or more complex curves. However, the sharpest part of the curve on the line will be the ruling radius, and this will determine what locos or stock will be able to pass through it.

Apart from this curve, an important consideration is the length of the switches, which can decide how rapidly a train will diverge from the straight path. The crossing angle is defined by a gradient, for example 1 in 10, and of course is the angle through the crossing. What is defined as the lead of the point depends on the crossing angle, and is the distance between the tip of the switch blade and the nose of the crossing. Usually the well-defined relationships between these hold. However, sometimes due to circumstances, the lead has to vary.

Apart from standard turnouts (points), there are curved points where both lines through the point curve in one direction. In so-called 'Y' points both lines diverge in opposite directions. Imagining a straight line through the centre of a 'Y' brings us to a three-way point.

LYNTON 009

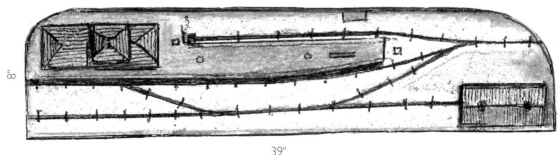

8"

39"

THIS PAGE:
Lynton layout and heading.

TOP: *Lynton station building. The goods shed is painted on the backscene.*

OPPOSITE PAGE:

BOTTOM LEFT: *View looking towards Exmoor, hand painted.*

BOTTOM RIGHT: *Hand-painted backscene. Track Peco 009.*

COMPLEX POINTS/ TURNOUTS

More complex formations include double slips and single slips. A double slip has basically the same function as two points end to end, only in one unit. Although a single slip looks similar to a double slip, its function is different. There is a basic crossover, but whereas it is possible to pass through, rather than cross over, on both lines on a double slip, on a single slip it is only possible to pass through on one side.

All these items of pointwork are available as 'ready-to-run' items. There are a lot of other track formations, but these would require making from scratch – often they were evolved for a particular situation and wouldn't find general use.

OPPOSITE PAGE:
TOP: The station building is card with embossed stone, and the tiles are card.

BOTTOM: Signal MSE etched brass and ratio.

THIS PAGE:
ABOVE: Lynton & Barnstaple train near the platform end.

LEFT: The station sign and two small buildings are scratch-built in card.

RAILS AND TRAIN WEIGHTS
RAIL CODES

Model rails are usually described by a code number: so, for example, code 100 means the rail height will be $^{100}/_{1,000}$in in height. The other dimensions of the rail will be in proportion. Usually these are based on those of a mainline rail shape. In '00' code, 100 is the height of the Peco Streamline 00 track. Code 75 is the usual choice for fine-scale track. Bullhead rail is code 75. Code 80 is used for commercial narrow-gauge track in 4mm scale. In 2mm scale code 80 is often used, and code 55 for 2mm fine scale.

The continental equivalent of 00, HO is a slightly smaller scale but uses the same gauge. We saw earlier that representing the standard gauge of 4ft 8½in using a scale of 3.5mm to one foot, is closer to scale than 00, which is narrow relative to the scale (4mm) dimension.

Small section rail, intended to represent heavy, mainline rail in a small scale, can be used to portray light or narrow gauge rail in a larger scale. Strictly speaking, rail proportions would probably not be correct for narrow-gauge rails, which generally have larger heads relative to their heights.

The size of full-size rails is usually described by the weight of a certain short length – for example, 80lb per yard. Cross-sections of rails have been traditionally described by a series of British Standards.

Not only narrow lines, but standard-gauge lines used light rails, and were often referred to as 'light railways'. Even some broad-gauge lines employed light rail sections, such as Irish 5ft 3in gauge lines. When vehicles have many wheels, to spread the loads, this can maximize the load-carrying capacity of a particular rail. However, the friction would be greater.

Of course, locos need to exert a certain amount of pressure on rails in terms of adhesive weight to pull a train without slipping. The weight of a train is not the only factor: friction in the bearings is another. Of course, the gradients will also define the loads that can be carried. To some extent, wheels can 'lose their feet' and slip if the rails are greasy. This can also happen if the weight on the driving wheels is not enough.

I saw a strange situation on a layout many years ago. The model had a terminus at the top of a 1-in-30 gradient. Tank engines could pull three bogie coaches up the bank and large tender locos could just about manage one! It turned out that the tender pick-up, for extra current collection, was bearing very tightly on the tender wheel backs, causing a lot of friction.

Friction is the rubbing effect caused when one surface slides over the other. Friction is dissipated as heat.

Track curves, of course, have an effect on vehicles passing through them. The momentum of a vehicle tends towards movement continuing in a straight line. Forward momentum becomes angular momentum on a curve, where the energy stored, due to a vehicle's weight (mass), acts to move it sideways – unlike energy that is dissipated in friction. Energy stored in an object when it is in motion tends to keep it moving when you try to bring it to a halt. This is why many mechanical devices that move need to have brakes. These are dissipating the formerly stored energy as heat and losing it, turning it into a different form that does not interfere with slowing down the train.

TRAIN WEIGHTS

From tests that have been done, it seems that weighting vehicles above a certain factor is counterproductive. One would think that a heavier vehicle would run more freely down a gradient, but the effect of the extra weight is almost exactly balanced by additional friction in the bearings. Any more weight than necessary will add more friction to the train and make gradients more difficult to pass over. Having said that, if the track is not too well laid, a bit of extra weight might help to keep a train from derailing – but obviously it is better to try to lay the track properly in the first place! Of course, weight on the wheels should be roughly the same throughout each vehicle (except for the loco or train power unit). The centre of gravity should be kept low – that is to say, weight is better low in a vehicle rather than near roof level.

It is not a good idea to mix light and heavier vehicles in a train, since the lighter vehicles may be lifted off the track going round the curves.

CHAPTER SEVEN

WIRING AND SOLDERING

Wiring is a subject that frightens many people contemplating building a model railway layout. But the same potential modellers are often quite happy driving cars or using computer systems and smart phones without having a clue about their inner workings! These days there are digital systems available to control model railway layouts that can be installed by following a simple set of instructions. You don't need arcane knowledge to fit and operate them, any more than a deep understanding of quantum physics is needed to build and operate a conventional DC layout.

If we keep to a few basic electrical rules we can do everything we need to do, and it will work. Besides, some basic knowledge is always a good thing – so here are some basic electricity rules, and hints and tips on how to wire up a layout.

WIRING DC LAYOUTS

Most model railways have two wires that feed to the two rails. When electricity is applied to the track a loco will travel either forwards or backwards, depending which way round the two wires are connected to the rails. So if there is a red wire and a black wire, if the red wire is connected to the left rail and the black wire to the right one, the train will travel in one direction. But if the wires were reversed and the red wire was connected to the right rail and the black wire to the left, the train would travel in the opposite direction. If a model railway controller is connected to the two wires, the other ends being attached to the rails as before, the controller should be able to alter the direction of the train. The controller 'controls' the flow of electricity to a train on the track, and is able to make it go faster or more slowly, as well as reverse its direction of travel.

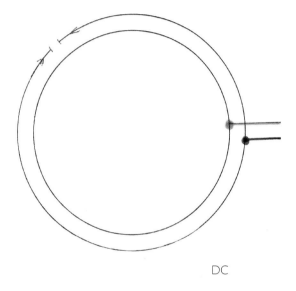

DC

Track circle with a break in one line, and electrical input to both lines.

A model railway motor will convert the electrical energy into a circular mechanical motion of the motor via an armature connected to the wheels by mechanical gears. To make a motor go faster or more slowly, it is easiest to imagine the controller supplying a greater or smaller amount of electricity to the motor of the wheels. In fact there are three quantities involved: voltage, current and resistance. These terms will be explained later.

If a controller is feeding electricity to a simple circle of track, a train will happily trundle round it in either direction, depending on the polarity of the rails. Reverse the polarity and the train will change direction.

If a break is made in one rail of the track, the electricity will still be able to reach either side of the break. If a break is made on the other rail too, the electric current

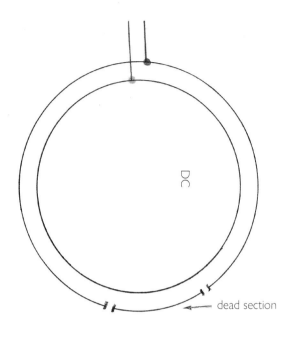

DC

dead section

DC

switch

Track circle with two breaks on one line, and electrical feed.

As left, but with a switch on the dead section.

will still be able to reach both sides. However, if a break were to be made on the same line so that there were two breaks one after the other on the same rail, the portion of rail between the two breaks would not be 'live'. In fact, this 'dead' section of track could be switched on and off by a suitable switch and length of wire connecting it to the live part of the rail.

This arrangement is called a 'switched dead section'. If it were situated as part of the siding (at the end) there would only be one insulated break.

Many points contain a switching facility to switch the line beyond, to be isolated or live depending on which way the point/turnout is set. These are known as isolating sections.

Suitable switches to switch dead sections on and off are called single-pole single-throw switches. If for some reason it is necessary to switch both rails on and off, the correct switch would be a double-pole single-throw switch. There are also double-throw switches, which move the electric signal from one pair of rails

to another. Isolating sections of one type or another is only really needed on the traditional DC layouts.

Digital control layouts do not need dead sections, or only where there is the possibility of power from one rail being able to reach the other rails, in which case there will be a short circuit (see below).

If there is a section of double track line with two points forming a crossing on it, with one controller feeding each track and an insulating break on each rail of the crossover (two points) between the two, lines will be needed. To cross over from one line to the other, for a train to pass across the crossover, it is necessary to set both controllers to the same speed and direction, and a train will run from one track to the other. For lines where there are more than two lines, the same arrangement can be multiplied up accordingly.

As a basic description, the above covers wiring needed for the DC analogue layout in terms of track feeds and insulated breaks.

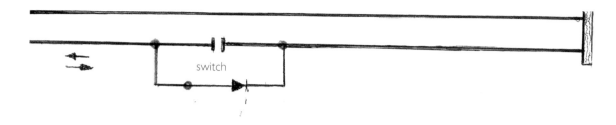

A switch on one line on a length of plain track.

*Electrical arrangement for a train
to cross from one line to another.*

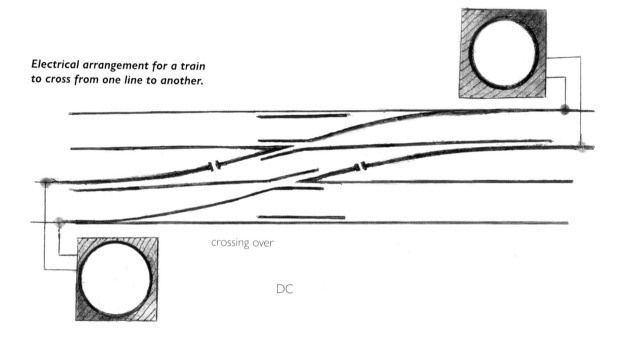

crossing over

DC

DCC AND DIGITAL CONTROL

The idea of digitally controlling model railways has been around for quite a few years. In the UK, Hornby set the ball rolling with their zero one system, which in spite of a few shortcomings worked quite well – there are still a few modellers using it. These days, digital control is a familiar part of the model railway scene.

The basic difference between digital control and how model railways were operated traditionally is that with a digital system an operator controls the individual trains, not the track. On a non-DCC layout the electricity is applied to the rails and a train moves. However, if there is a train already on the track, it will move too. Independent control is impossible unless trains occupy independent tracks fed from independent controllers.

With DCC, trains can be moved individually even though the track is always live and other trains are on it. If a train is selected, it is the only one that will move, unless another train has been 'logged in', in which case that will move too, but can be independently controlled. In addition, train lights can be switched on and off, and authentic prototype train sounds reproduced from a small loudspeaker in the train or loco.

WIRING A DCC LAYOUT

In wiring terms, the difference between a traditional DC layout and a digital one is that on the latter all tracks are live – there are no dead sections to store stationary trains or individual locos. Digital trains are all controlled from the digital controller.

In theory you only need two wires to feed a digital layout. Well, you can run a traditional DC layout with just two wires, but things can get rather more complicated! With DCC you can plug everything you need into the track, including point motors – as long as each element has its own digital identity, this is possible. But some modellers prefer to operate their points using basically an analogue system, not physically connected to the digital system. It is certainly easier to fault find if point control, signals and so on have separate circuits.

On large layouts extra feeds around the layout are really worthwhile to avoid voltage drop, which can happen quite easily across fishplates.

If your experience has been the same as mine, packets of metal fishplates come in three types of supposedly the same type – those that are loose, those that are too tight and those that are just right. It is easy to deal with the loose ones – just give them a few gentle taps with a small hammer. Tight ones are too fiddly to bother with. In digital (DCC), poor electrical connections are bad news.

LIVE AND DEAD FROG POINTS/TURNOUTS

For some strange reason the middle crossing area of a point/turnout has come to be called a 'frog' on model railway points/turnouts. I have already covered points (turnouts) that can isolate sidings beyond the 'frog' (the area round the 'crossing nose') electrically. In full size railway terminology, it is partly plastic, therefore insulated, which makes it a dead frog! There is a live frog too, which is metal. This rather bizarre terminology of live and dead frogs prompted one of the track manufacturers to call these 'insulfrog' and 'electrofrog' respectively!

Both of these point types can isolate sidings beyond because the power for the sidings is dependent on which way the point blades (switch tongues) are

set and make contact with the stock rails alongside. The problem with this arrangement is that you need to keep the edges of the blades clean, and also the parts of the stock rails with which the blades make contact: the contact between them must be good. Dirty contacts are a common problem on layouts, causing the current from the rails to the trains to be interrupted.

Of course, on a digital layout there is no need for the lines beyond the crossing nose (frog) to be isolated. 'Jumper leads' of thin wire can be fitted between the point blades and the adjacent stock rails. The points need to be insulfrog points (plastic frog). After this treatment there is no further need to clean the point blades (switches). However, don't try this treatment with electrofrog points.

So why use live frog points? On these there is more live contact between the wheels and the rails than on the insulfrog type of point (turnout). When a loco has only a few wheels with which to pick up the current, and when slow running through points (turnouts) is very important, there is a good case for using electrofrog-type points. However, most locos will negotiate the dead frog points currently available, even set-track ones – but when a baseboard is not flat, small variations in the rail heights may cause wheels to lose contact with the tracks momentarily. This might be more of a problem with insulfrog points because of any 'insul' areas.

SHORT CIRCUITS

I mentioned earlier that it is important to prevent areas of opposite polarity making contact with one another. This is particularly important with a digital layout because contact of even a very short duration can cause system protection circuits to activate to protect the sensitive electronics. Analogue traditional layouts are not so sensitive. This situation is described as a short circuit.

Electricity consists of current, voltage and resistance. Current is the rate at which electric charge flows through a circuit, whereas voltage is a measure of how strong it is. The greater the difference in the amount of electric energy between two places in an electrical circuit, the higher the voltage (or the difference in potential). This is rather like water moving through a pipe. The amount of water flowing is like a current in a wire, whereas voltage is the force of the water flowing past a particular point. If a short has occurred, and if protection circuits detect it, the circuit won't turn on again until the source of the short is dealt with.

Resistance goes with current and voltage. Resistance is whatever resists the flow of electricity. It is measured in ohms, whereas current it measured in amps (milliamps) and volts (millivolts). When an electric motor in a train is in the circuit, this will offer resistance to the flow of the current. Without this the only limiting resistance would be the wire and rails, which have little resistance. So if by accident a direct link is made across the rails, the electricity will take the path of least resistance, forming a short circuit. In theory a large current will flow, but in practice a protection circuit should switch off the current. 'Shorts' are a problem because it is not always easy to spot their source.

WIRING A LAYOUT

There are ways of wiring layouts without soldering, but the most effective method of making connections is by soldering. This is covered in the next section. Generally speaking, wires are beneath baseboards, rather than above them. Any battens under the boards can be traversed by drilling holes though which wires can be passed. Drilling these is one of the first jobs in the wiring process once the wiring paths have been decided on. Any extra ones can be added later, but once some wiring is in place there is always the possibility of inadvertently drilling through a batten with a bunch of wires behind it!

A good way of fixing wiring to boards is with tie wraps and 'stickies' – the self-adhesive bases through which plastic ties are threaded. Then the ties are wound round the wires they are going to secure. When fixing the stickies to a baseboard it is best to use an extra impact adhesive on the sticky bases to secure them, otherwise the weight of the wires will pull the bases away from the baseboards over a matter of time.

FITTING POINT MOTORS

If you intend to use point motors to operate the points that are under the baseboards and are therefore hidden from view, these usually have a pin that, when the point motor is in place, passes upwards through a hole drilled in the baseboard and into a small hole in the tie bar of the point. It is worth drilling the holes before the points are fixed down. I find it is easiest to pin the points down loosely, hold the point tie bar in the middle of its throw, and drill a hole slightly smaller than the bar hole. All that is needed is to mark the position on the baseboard where the hole is going to be. If the point (turnout) is then unpinned and removed, the full-size hole can be drilled to give clearance for the operating pin to move. I drill a 6mm hole for the 00-gauge 4mm-scale point. Smaller gauge point holes can be a smaller size.

Once the larger hole is drilled out, and once track laying is complete, I start adding the point motors. It is useful to secure the motors first with impact adhesive, as this allows for them to be moved around a little to find the best position with the pin in place in the tie-bar hole. Then it can be pressed firmly in place and the adhesive allowed to dry. If required, small screws can be added once the ideal position for the tie-point motor has been found, and has been glued in place. This way of fitting point motors is particularly useful if you have to work under the baseboard to fit the motors.

Incidentally, it is easier to work on baseboards – fitting point motors, turning up – with them vertical, prior to the boards being connected together. The boards can be clamped in this position. This is much more comfortable than fumbling around trying to reach up under the boards when they are already in place. Of course, if the baseboards *are* already in place then there is no alternative.

SOLENOID POINT MOTORS (PECO, SEEP)

Solenoid point motors of the type being fitted here consist of two coils of wire through which a single steel rod passes. When an electric current is fed to each coil in turn, the rod will be propelled first one way and then the other by the magnetic force generated by the coils and the current flowing through

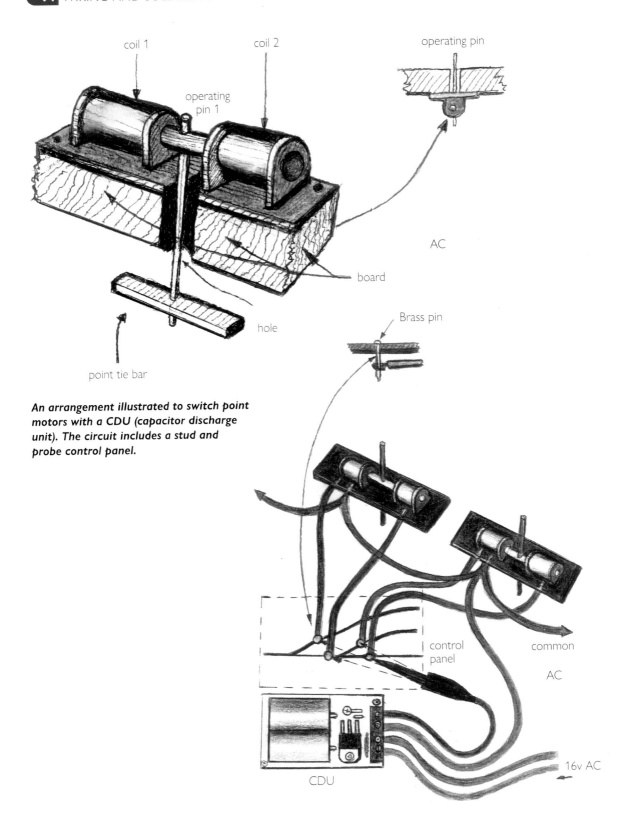

coil 1

coil 2

operating pin

operating pin 1

AC

board

hole

point tie bar

An arrangement illustrated to switch point motors with a CDU (capacitor discharge unit). The circuit includes a stud and probe control panel.

Brass pin

control panel

common

AC

16v AC

CDU

FLOATING POINTS AND MOTORS

A system once advocated by Peco involved fixing their point motors to the base of the points, making holes for the point motor in the baseboard. The whole track point motor assemblage floated effectively on foam underlay. The system isolated the track vibration transmitted by the train from getting through to the baseboard, which, as we have seen, can be a very effective sounding board. In the example of this technique that I saw the foam underlay had unfortunately rotted: in this syndrome the foam disintegrates with age, either becoming like glue or crumbling. Foam cone surrounds on loudspeakers suffer a similar fate.

them. This is a simple method of switching points and is very reliable in practice – although for some reason the SEEP type operating pins dropped out occasionally if the pins were not fixed securely. However, this hasn't been a problem for some time.

One problem with point motors is that their action is quite violent, although often this is positively an advantage because it can overcome any stickiness caused by slight misalignment of point motors. If this type of motor is used for other operations their forceful action can be almost an embarrassment. I once used one to energize a '0'-gauge signal – at a model railway show the signal arm shot into space and landed two stands away.

SLOW-ACTING POINT MOTORS

Some points need a less forceful action, and some modellers prefer motors with a gentler movement. In this case so-called slow-acting point motors can be used. These create a slower movement, and some modellers like them just for the realism this affords. Certainly points/turnouts that have more delicate moving parts need a gentle touch. For example, the slightly bullish solenoid motors are not ideal where thin point tie bars use printed circuit board: the blades

are soldered to the copper face of the tie bars, and come adrift when the soldered joints break.

Generally, slower action point/turnout motors use a conventional motor geared down.

A NUMBER OF POINT MOTORS 'FIRING' TOGETHER

One problem with solenoid motors is when a number of points are 'fired' together and are wired together in what is known as 'parallel' (if they are linked together one after the other, this is known as wiring in series). Parallel wiring means that more current is flowing, and the motors use up the electric discharge of the CDU more quickly than the single motor. Mechanically these point motors do not respond at the same rate as one another, so if one lags behind, the others may have soaked up the current before it has moved, so that particular point won't throw. This in fact might happen in several motors in a group 'thrown' together.

Smart Switches

The system known as smart switches operates points using servos. Servos have been used with radio-controlled planes for some years. With digital control, servos can be set up to have predetermined throws, and the speeds of operation can also be pre-arranged.

THE RETURN LOOP

Whether we are talking about digital or DC wiring, basic track plans can apply to either. One such arrangement that can catch out modellers of both is the return loop: this is simply a loop of track that starts from a straight section and runs round and back on itself. In doing this the rails reverse – effectively the left rail loops round and in doing this joins up with the right rail, inevitably causing a short circuit on a layout. A switchable dead section on the loop needs to be fitted, on which the polarity of the track can be reversed to match the first straight section ahead.

DCC INDEPENDENT CONTROL OF TRAINS

On a DCC digital layout a special reversing module can be fitted to accomplish the same thing regarding the reversing loop. A similar problem could occur with a return loop that bisects an oval of track, creating two return loops.

One of the great advantages of digital control is being able to have a number of trains occupying the same line, which can be controlled independently. This can be done with traditional control, to some extent, by splitting up a line into a number of sections isolated from one another. Each section is switchable to a number of controllers, and each controller can be connected in turn to the

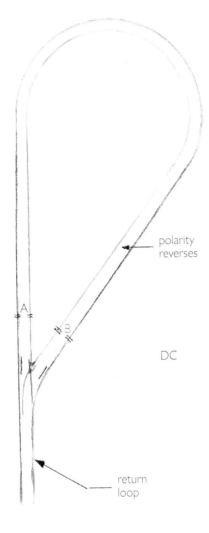

polarity reverses

DC

A

B

return loop

ABOVE: A return loop.

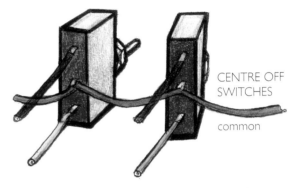

CENTRE OFF SWITCHES

common

*ABOVE: **Two spring-centre off switches, operation wired to operate point motors.***

MOMENTARY TOGGLE SWITCHES

SPDT SWITCH

DPDT SWITCH

SPST SWITCH

*RIGHT: **Three switch types and how they are portrayed diagrammatically.***

*MIDDLE RIGHT: **Second switch, as above.***

*FAR RIGHT: **Third switch, as above.***

SINGLE POLE DOUBLE THROW

DOUBLE POLE DOUBLE THROW

on

off

SINGLE POLE SINGLE THROW

sections consecutively. This means that several trains can follow each other down the layout. This can work quite effectively, and usually uses rotary switches. A layout configured this way is of course quite complex to wire, whereas achieving the same aim with digital control is much simpler and ultimately more effective.

Before leaving this overview of model railway wiring, we should return to electrofrog and insulfrog points. When using electrofrog points/turnouts, if power can reach both sides of the point, the point blade can cause a direct connection between the live frog and the stock rails and cause a short circuit. So don't throw all your plastic insulating fishplates away just because you have gone digital!

STUD AND PROBE CONTROL PANELS

Digitally controlled layouts can have points controlled via the digital system; analogue DC layouts will usually need a control panel. A simple method of arranging this is to have a track plan of the layout mounted on a board that is drilled to have brass pins following the diagram, two for every point (left/right). The pins are wired into the point motor circuit, so electrical DC power is fed to the pins via a metal probe, which is wired to the system; it completes the circuit when it is touched to a pin, which 'throws' the point. This is a very simple and effective way of controlling points; otherwise switches can be used.

SOLDERING

Soldering is one of those subjects that seem to invoke fear in people and an immediate response that 'I could

never do that'. Actually, it is quite easy to get the hang of soldering if you remember a few simple rules. The first is to keep the soldering iron bit clean, and the second is to make sure that the area you want to solder is kept hot enough to melt the solder properly. The solder you use is also important, and the process won't work unless there is a flux. Flux enables the solder to fix itself to whatever it is you are soldering. The solder we are most familiar with has cores of flux in it. These are fine for most jobs; usually these fluxes are inert, which means they are only active when they are hot, and usually burn off. Others can stay active and cause corrosion if they are not cleaned off. Cored solders are fine for trackwork and most other jobs.

Sometimes low melting-point solders are used: these melt at a lower temperature than cored solders, and are useful when you want to solder an additional part of something that has been already soldered, without unsoldering the part that has been soldered already. Low melting-point solders are also used to solder white-metal kits and parts, which have a relatively low melting point themselves.

TINNING THE IRON

Tinning the iron is a very important process. The solder needs to be held against a bit as it heats up. As soon as it melts the solder, it needs to be moved across the bit so that the solder melts everywhere on the face. Then a damp sponge needs to be wiped across the bit. The face of the bit should now be covered in a layer of solder. Once more solder is applied, the iron is ready. This operation needs to be carried out fairly often to prevent the surface oxidizing, as this will reject the solder.

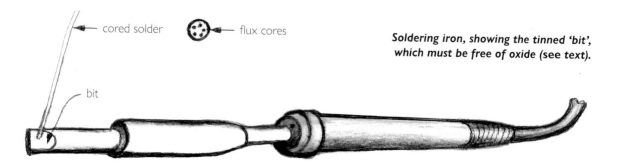

cored solder   flux cores

bit

Soldering iron, showing the tinned 'bit', which must be free of oxide (see text).

SOLDERING WIRES TO THE TRACK

Hold the hot tinned bit against the rail, then add the solder as the iron heats up the rail. Once the feed wire has been tinned this can then be soldered to the tinned rail.

When soldering bulky objects, brass and nickel solders are more likely to be used: these dissipate heat very quickly away from the heat source (the iron). This means that a fairly large soldering iron will be required to do the job. It is best to try to support the parts to be soldered with some kind of jig, however apparently crude, as the soldered areas are likely to be become very hot and impossible to hold. Always apply the heat from the iron to the material, then touch the solder to the latter and wait until it melts.

The priority in this section is to describe the basics of soldering and stress what is important. It is not difficult to learn to solder, and once you have learnt how to do this you will wonder how you managed to do railway modelling without being able to solder before. Remember, always keep the bit clean and the areas to be soldered, by scraping the surface. Make sure you have enough heat. If you do use additional liquid flux in addition to that in the solder cores, make sure the two are compatible.

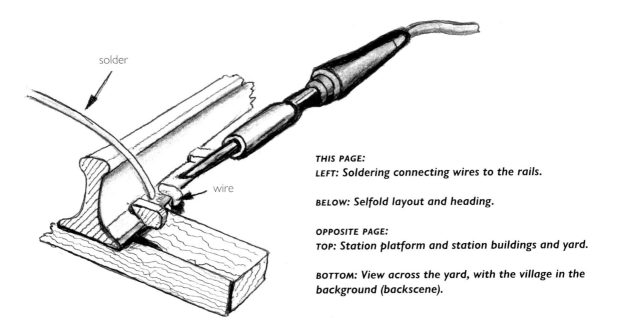

solder

wire

THIS PAGE:

LEFT: *Soldering connecting wires to the rails.*

BELOW: *Selfold layout and heading.*

OPPOSITE PAGE:

TOP: *Station platform and station buildings and yard.*

BOTTOM: *View across the yard, with the village in the background (backscene).*

SELFOLD 00

12"

54"

Signal box based on one at Midhurst, made from scratch-built plastic card.

Standard 2MT tack loco (Bachmann), with the village beyond.

Bullied pacific loco (Hornby) runs round its train.

The earlier period portrayed H class and T9 (Hornby) locos.

CHAPTER EIGHT

BALLASTING TRACK AND WEATHERING

The trouble with ballasting model railway track is that you can't just pour ballasting on the track: you have to do it carefully, otherwise it looks horrible. If you have a lot of ballasting to do, the task can get quite tedious. Still, well ballasted track looks very good, and it is worth the trouble. Over the years I have tried to make this more time-consuming of activities easier. I made plasticard devices that made the outside of the ballast the correct shape while going round curves. This worked quite well, but the plasticard blade wore out very quickly. Then I made little cardboard troughs that could be filled with ballast, which when pulled across the sleepers dropped ballast between the rails.

In the end, the easiest ballasting technique was to take up a small amount of ballast at a time and dribble it between my fingers into the gaps between the sleepers; like this you have very good control over the flow of the ballast, though it is still time-consuming.

Once the ballast is in place it can be glued down with a mixture of adhesive and water, plus a little washing-up liquid to break the surface tension of the liquid and let it flow easily. There are many model ballasts. I tend to steer clear of the ones that aren't miniature stone chippings but are plastic, as these tend to float on the glue and make ballasting more difficult. To apply the glue, eye droppers work well – PVA glue is a common choice as the adhesive.

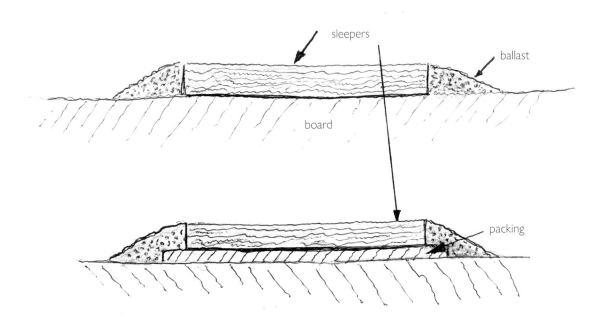

Ballast and sleeper depths.

A ballasting trough. Folded thin card trough made to carry ballast; a little ballast is dropped between each sleeper as the trough bumps along the sleeper tops. Different sizes of trough are needed.

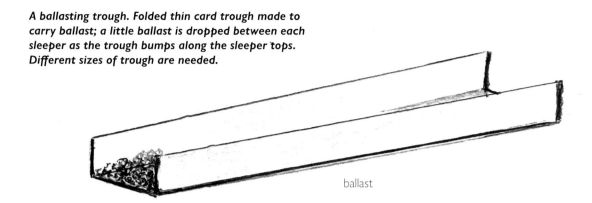

ballast

WEATHERING TRACK AND LINESIDE OBJECTS

It is always surprising how many potions are available for weathering models – track included. However, for most modellers these are needed because taking paint from tins and bottles to replicate the shades of weathering makes the job much easier. My approach is rather different. Because I learned about paints at art college, I tend to mix the colour with a very basic set of artist's colours: raw sienna, burnt sienna, plus black and white. The two siennas are so-called earth colours, the pigment being originally derived from iron oxides. These will be instantly recognizable as the colours of rust. Also, bricks and tiles will show the same colours.

If you mix raw sienna, black and white you can make a convincing concrete colour; adding more raw sienna gives it the look of concrete with more sand in the mix. It all boils down to the choice of colours and the mixing. You won't want to use much black, as black is quickly overpowering. If a little black is added to white, grey is the result – which is not like weathered tones either.

The answer to weathering is to experiment. One approved method is dry brushing, where most of the paint is removed by rubbing until you really have to scrub hard with a paintbrush to deposit any paint on the object. This is good for subtle weathering. Air brushes are good for weathering, but it is hard to produce effects where an object doesn't look as if it has been airbrushed.

If you take the colours I suggested for concrete (actually black and white aren't colours) you might find that applying the paint thinly to various objects creates a realistic effect. Try dry brushing too, adding a little burnt sienna where there is obvious rust.

When it comes to track colour, I always remember waiting to change trains and looking at the rails in an adjacent yard – and no two seemed to be quite the same in colours and tones.

For track in general, commercial track colours plus a little weathering will create a good effect. Sleepers again benefit from concrete tones. Dry brush across them and this will show up the wood grain – if they have it.

FOLLOWING PAGES:

P.104:
A large N-gauge layout built by Allen Etheridge and the author.

P.105:
TOP: The Swiss/International.

BOTTOM: Layout shown in Chapter 3, under construction.

CHAPTER NINE

SCRATCH-BUILT TRACK

There are situations where suitable track systems are not available – for example where there is an unusual gauge, or a modeller might feel he can produce more realistic trackwork than is available from the trade. In these circumstances scratch-building tracks is the answer – though some modellers just like making it themselves, of course!

In the past, making your own track was the only way, and it is strange to reflect that to build a relatively scale-looking model railway, you had to make almost everything yourself. It is fair to assume that anyone making track by hand has had previous experience of track laying flexible or sectional track. I have assumed that this is the case.

The simplest of track formations is the straight length of track. Everything would be simple if all track were straight, but the moment you go round a curve, things get much harder. Momentum tries to keep the train going in a straight line, and you get angular momentum you didn't have on the straight. If you have a switched system (point/turnout) to move from a straight line to a curve, or vice versa, then there are quite a few things to think about.

Actually, we have looked at how points work and what they consist of, and there are also vital statistics. So, when you make a point/turnout, if you keep to the inter-related dimensions related to the wheels sets you have in use, then things should be fine. Making a point is therefore down to accuracies of key dimensions, in particular how well you make the parts needed. In fact there aren't that many parts that need to be made, as such; the crossing nose requires filing or machining, point blades/switch tongues need to be shaped out of rail to bed against the stock rails, and the rest is shaping rails into a curve, or bending rails.

The related skills are few. Being able to file pieces of metal accurately is important, but like all these things, it is straightforward if you proceed in a certain manner (of course this has to be the right manner!). Accurate measuring is important. You'll need track gauges to make pointwork, which grip the rails to give the right clearances.

If you are making track to existing standards, for example, EM or P4 gauge, the societies relevant to these are well worth joining, for all sorts of reasons, but they will probably be able to provide you with gauges to suit their particular standards. Of course, if your intention is to model Etruscan Broad gauge you might find that you are on your own! An obvious point is to obtain track diagrams for something to copy. The best are the scale drawings from the railway company sources. It is not a good idea to take measurements off drawings reworked for your particular scale. Rather, derive your dimensions from those marked on the drawings. Model flangeway clearances are usually overscale, due to how narrow they become when reduced down in scale to model sizes, at least in the smaller scales. In P4 scale the clearance in 4mm scale is fairly close, EM slightly less so, and so on. Whatever the track standards, their associated wheel standards are important to observe.

PRODUCING SCRATCH-BUILT TRACK

The following is a description of how to undertake the various operations needed to produce scratch-built track.

The first thing to do is to produce a template for every item of track you want. This can be on paper,

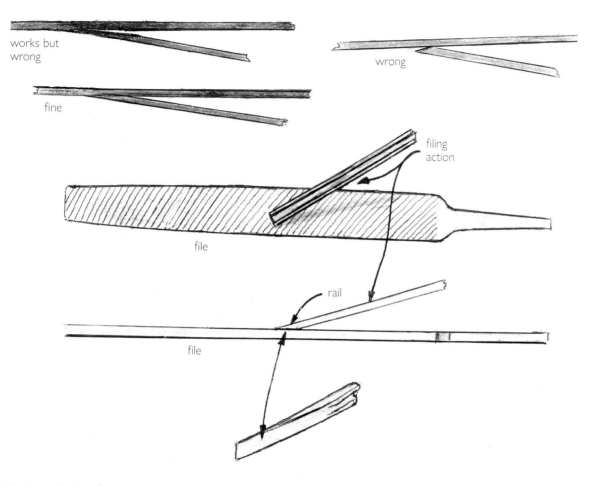

Track making – preparing the rails – filing.

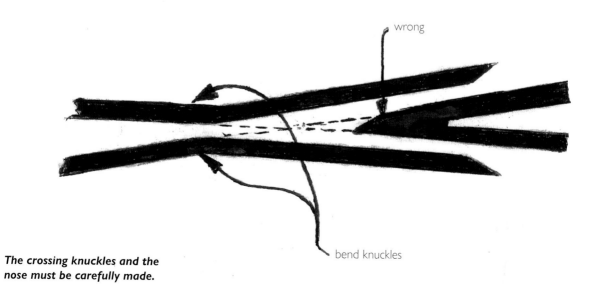

The crossing knuckles and the nose must be carefully made.

and the templates can be stuck down to a more solid surface – baseboard, or whichever. First draw a centreline and the two running lines to connect the distance apart for the chosen gauge. The same applies to drawing up points, but only two lines are drawn, the straight line and the diverging line; the angle between this and the first line is the crossing angle. The curve between the two parts of the stock rail can be drawn in. Often this can be a single radius curve.

The curved rail on the other side to the closure rail or closure can be drawn to follow the first. We have what is known as a natural angle turnout: this is based round a segment of a circle that starts with a tangent to the through line, and ends in a tangent with the straight line of the crossing, for freedom of movement for the wheels.

When it comes to making up the point/turnout, the gauge can be set by track gauges, which grip the rails while these are fixed down. The same goes for check rails and for creating gauge widening on the curves. So the drawing is a basic guide.

Sleepers are available from various sources. A useful technique is to use copper-clad sleepers to which the rails can be soldered. I mentioned this in relation to making bullhead rail track earlier. Flat-bottom rail can be soldered to the sleepers in the same manner, giving the look of flat-bottomed track. By using suitable sleeper lengths, broad- or narrow-gauge trackwork can be produced.

Probably this sort of trackwork, with copper-clad sleepers, is the easiest to make, visually. Its main shortcoming is its lack of wood effect on the sleepers, which of course you would get with wooden sleepers. But once the track is weathered this won't really be noticeable.

If soldering is subtly done there are no obvious rail fixings – though cosmetic fixings can be added, of course. But whichever type of construction technique you use, you need to be fairly adept at soldering.

If you start with making copper-clad track, the experience will give you a mastery of the techniques you will need in any area of bespoke track making.

APPENDIX

GAUGES AND SCALES

MOST POPULAR SCALES STANDARD GAUGE

Scale	Millimetres mm/ft	Ratio	Prototype	Gauge
N UK	2.062	1:148	4ft 8½in	9mm
N ABROAD	2	1:160	4ft 8½in	9mm
HO	3.5	1:87	4ft 8½in	16.5mm
00	4	1:76	4ft 8½in	16.5mm

LESS FAMILIAR SCALES

Scale	Millimetres mm/ft	Ratio	Prototype	Gauge
Z	1.5	1:203	4ft 8½in	6.5mm

LARGER SCALES

Scale	Millimetres mm/ft	Ratio	Prototype	Gauge
0	17	1:43.5	4ft 8½in	32mm
1	10	1:30	4ft 8½in	45mm

NARROW-GAUGE SCALES

Scale	Millimetres mm/ft	Ratio	Prototype	Gauge
N–6.5	2.062	1:148	3ft 00in	1.5mm
HO M	3.5	1:87	1m	12mm
HO n 3	3.5	1:87	3ft 00in	10.5mm
009	4	1:76	2ft 3in	9mm
0 – 16.5	7	1:43.5	2ft 4½in	16.5mm
SG – 45	13.5	1:22.5	1m	45mm
SM32	16	1:19	2ft	32mm

4mm SCALES STANDARD CLOSER TO SCALE GAUGE

Scale	Millimetres mm/ft	Ratio	Prototype	Gauge
P4	4	1:76	4ft 8½in	18.83mm
EM	4	1:76	4ft 8½in	18.2mm

INDEX

Magical
Mathematical
Properties

Lisa Arias

rourkeeducationalmedia.com

Before Reading:

Building Academic Vocabulary and Background Knowledge

Before reading a book, it is important to tap into what your child or students already know about the topic. This will help them develop their vocabulary, increase their reading comprehension, and make connections across the curriculum.

1. *Look at the cover of the book. What will this book be about?*
2. *What do you already know about the topic?*
3. *Let's study the Table of Contents. What will you learn about in the book's chapters?*
4. *What would you like to learn about this topic? Do you think you might learn about it from this book? Why or why not?*
5. *Use a reading journal to write about your knowledge of this topic. Record what you already know about the topic and what you hope to learn about the topic.*
6. *Read the book.*
7. *In your reading journal, record what you learned about the topic and your response to the book.*
8. *After reading the book complete the activities below.*

Content Area Vocabulary

Read the list. What do these words mean?

associate
commutative property
    of addition
digit
distributive property
factor
identity property of
    addition
multiplication property
    of one
multiplication property
    of zero
operations
parenthesis
product
properties
sum

After Reading:

Comprehension and Extension Activity

After reading the book, work on the following questions with your child or students in order to check their level of reading comprehension and content mastery.

1. *What happens when you multiply a number by zero? What happens when you add a number to zero? (Summarize)*
2. *Why does the number order matter for subtraction and division but not multiplication and addition? (Infer)*
3. *Why are parenthesis so important in math? (Asking questions)*
4. *How does the distributive property help you add and multiply large numbers? (Asking questions)*
5. *What is the rule if you multiply a number by 1? (Summarize)*

Extension Activity

To learn more about the commutative property you will need 10 pennies and your hands. The commutative property states that no matter what order you add the numbers you will always get the same answer. Let's test this property! Using the 10 pennies split them up between your two hands. If you have 3 pennies in one hand and 7 in the other, how many total pennies do you have? What if you put 4 pennies in one hand and 6 pennies in the other? Keep trying different combinations!

Table of Contents

Numbers, Numbers Everywhere!

Operations join numbers together by allowing us to add, subtract, multiply, and divide.

Without operations, numbers would be left sitting side by side.

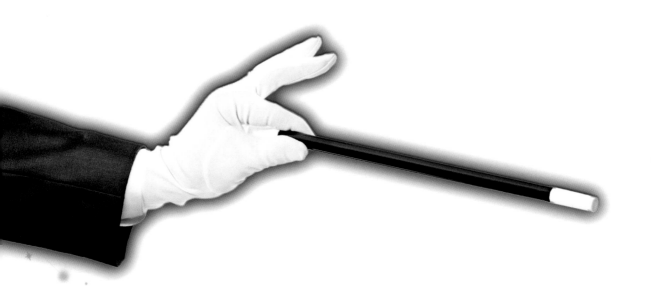

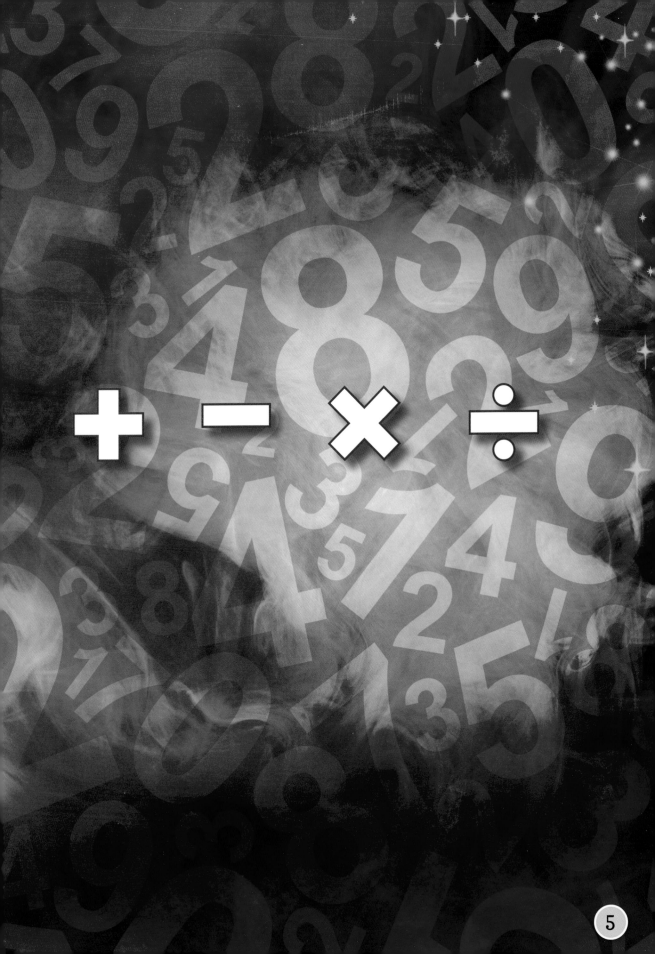

Properties

Instead of working out every math problem, **properties** help you calculate answers quickly in your head. They are the special rules that numbers follow.

Properties are useful to know and will help your math skills grow.

Commutative Associative Distributive

Commutative Property

The commutative property is where we will begin.
Adding or multiplying numbers in any order is a win!

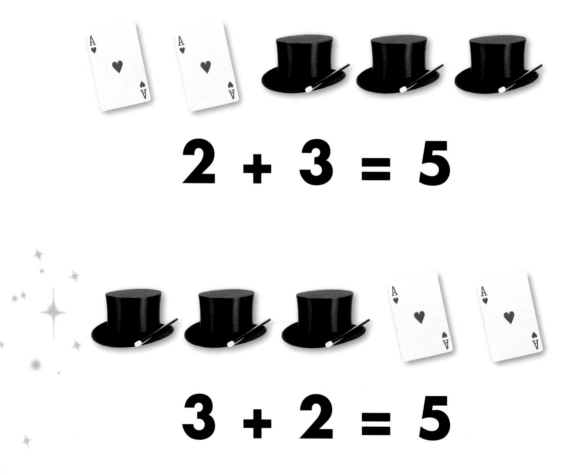

$$2 + 3 = 5$$

$$3 + 2 = 5$$

2 × 3 = 6

3 × 2 = 6

Commutative Property of Addition

The **commutative property of addition** falls into play when adding many numbers at once comes your way.

$$\mathbf{5} + 3 + \mathbf{5}$$

$$3 + \mathbf{10} = 13$$

Add the 5s first because making 10 is such a quick combination. Next, add the 3 and you have just used the commutative property!

$$1 + \mathbf{4} + \mathbf{4}$$

$$1 + \mathbf{8}$$

Add the doubles first to equal 8. Next add the 1 and you are done!

Add using the commutative property of addition.

1 + **5** + **5** + **5**

4 + 2 + **4**

10 + 8 + **10**

3 + 2 + **3**

Add Two-Digit Numbers

You will soon agree, using the commutative property to add two-**digit** numbers comes in quite handy.

$$21 + 13$$

21 → 20 1   13 → 10 3

$$20 + 10 = 30 \qquad 1 + 3 = 4$$

$$30 + 4 = 34$$

$$54 + 55$$

54 → 50 4   55 → 50 5

$$50 + 50 = 100 \qquad 4 + 5 = 9$$

$$100 + 9 = 109$$

First add the 10s and then add the 1s.

Add using the commutative property of addition.

72 + 25

44 + 51

28 + 12

66 + 22

Subtraction Restrictions

Addition and multiplication
follow the commutative property to perfection.

Subtraction, on the other hand,
can never be part of the plan.

$$8 - 5 = 3$$

$$5 - 8 \neq 3$$

?? ? ?

7 − 5 = 2

5 − 7 ≠ 2

 **? ?**

Always subtract in the order given.

Parenthesis are grouping symbols and are very wise.
They allow groups they **associate** to stay organized.

No need to complain, no matter the grouping, the answer remains.

Associative Property of Addition

$$(2 + 3) + 4 = 2 + (3 + 4)$$

Do First   Do First

$5 + 4 = 9$ is the
same as $2 + 7 = 9$

Associative Property of Multiplication

$$3 \times (4 \times 2) = (3 \times 4) \times 2$$

Do First   Do First

$$3 \times 8 = 24 \quad \text{is the same as} \quad 12 \times 2 = 24$$

Find each **sum** and as a bonus rewrite each expression using the associative property.

$$(4 + 5) + 3$$

$$8 + (2 + 4)$$

$$(6 + 7) + 5$$

$$10 + (7 + 2)$$

Rewritten using the associative property:

$$4 + (5 + 3)$$

$$(8 + 2) + 4$$

$$6 + (7 + 5)$$

$$(10 + 7) + 2$$

Find each **product** and as a bonus rewrite using the associative property.

$(3 \times 2) \times 5$

$9 \times (6 \times 1)$

$(10 \times 3) \times 3$

$4 \times (3 \times 4)$

Rewritten using the associative property:

$3 \times (2 \times 5)$

$(9 \times 6) \times 1$

$10 \times (3 \times 3)$

$(4 \times 3) \times 4$

Answers: 30 54 90 48

Distributive Property

If you run into trouble with a multiplication fact,
the **distributive property** will get you back on track.

Using the distributive property is smart.
It allows you to break factors into smaller parts.

15 × 5 Pick either **factor** to break apart.

15

Break apart **15**. ⟶ **10 + 5**

Multiply the new factors by 5. ⟶ **10 × 5** and **5 × 5**

Add the products. ⟶ **50 + 25 = 75**

The problem is done
when you find the sum!

12 × 6

12

Break apart **12**. If it works for you, try **10** and **2**.

Multiply the new factors by 6. → **10 × 6** and **2 × 6**

Add the products. → **60 + 12 = 72**

The problem is done when you find the sum!

Time to get serious with some more factor practice.

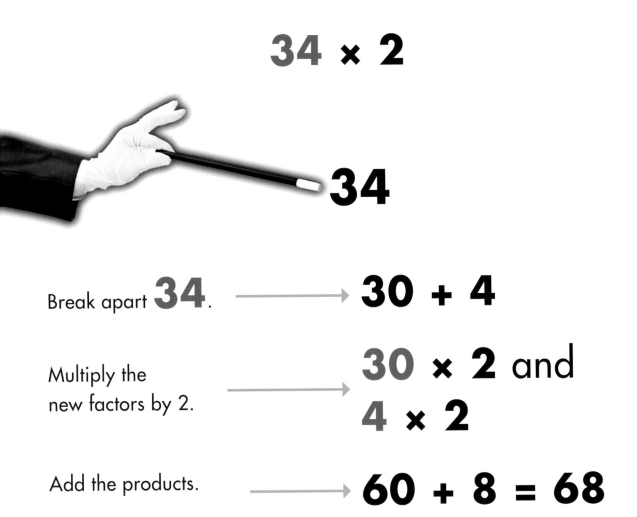

$$34 \times 2$$

34

Break apart **34**. ⟶ **30 + 4**

Multiply the
new factors by 2. ⟶ **30 × 2** and
4 × 2

Add the products. ⟶ **60 + 8 = 68**

The problem is done
when you find the sum!

65 × 3

101 × 9

88 × 5

44 × 6

Identity Property of Addition

Look in the mirror and you will see how the **identity property of addition** completes its mission: Any number plus zero will equal that number.

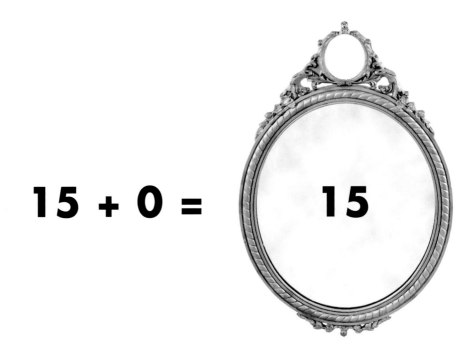

15 + 0 = **15**

Multiplication Property of One

Check the mirror again for the **multiplication property of one**:
Any number multiplied by one will equal that number.

223 × 1 = 223

Zero Property of Multiplication

We have saved the best for last.
The **multiplication property of zero** is a blast.

It is really easy to know.
Zero times any number equals zero.

$$3 \times 0 = 0$$

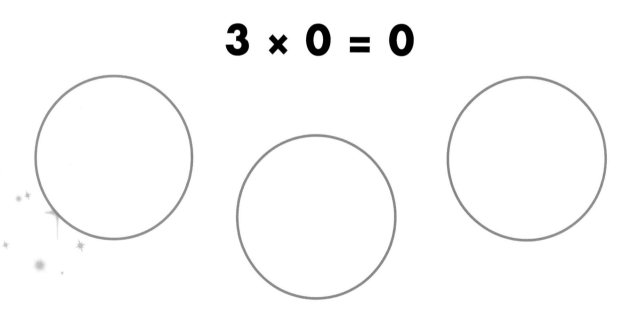

3 groups with 0 objects in each group.

No matter the number, big or small, this is always true.
Thanks to the multiplication property of zero rule.

$$2 \times 0 = 0$$

$$0 \times 0 = 0$$

$$0 \times 1,000,000 = 0$$

Name the Property

Show what you know, and name the correct property!

Word Bank

Commutative Property of Multiplication

Commutative Property of Addition

Associative Property

Distributive Property

Identity Property of Addition

Multiplication Property of One

Zero Property of Multiplication

None

$$15 \times 0 = 0$$

$$3 + 4 = 4 + 3$$

$$25 \times 6 = (20 \times 6) + (5 \times 6)$$

$$(7 + 8) + 9 = 7 + (8 + 9)$$

$$99 + 0 = 99$$

$$7 \times 8 = 8 \times 7$$

$$31 - 5 = 5 - 31$$

$$625 \times 1 = 625$$

Multiplication Property of One

None

Commutative Property of Multiplication

Identity Property of Addition

Associative Property

Distributive Property

Commutative Property of Addition

Zero Property of Multiplication

Answers:

29

Glossary

associate (uh-SOH-shee-eyt): to unite or combine

commutative property of addition (kuh-MYOO-tuh-tiv PROP-ur-tee uhv uh-DISH-uhn): if the order or the addends change, the sum remains the same

digit (DIJ-it): a written symbol for any numbers 0 to 9

distributive property (diss-TRIB-yoo-tiv prop-ur-tee): the product remains the same if you multiply a product by a product or by the sum of a product's addends

factor (FAK-tur): the number or numbers that are multiplied together

identity property of addition (eye-DEN-ti-tee prop-ur-tee uhv uh-DISH-uhn): any number plus zero equals that number

multiplication property of one (muhl-tuh-pli-KEY-shuhn PROP-ur-tee uhv wuhn): multiplying any number by one equals that number

multiplication property of zero (muhl-tuh-pli-KEY-shuhn PROP-ur-tee uhv ZEER-oh): multiplying any number by zero equals zero

operations (op-uh-RAY-shuhnz): a mathematical action that changes a number

parenthesis (puh-REN-thuh-siss): a set of curved lines () used for grouping in math

product (PROD-uhkt): the answer to a multiplication problem

properties (PROP-ur-teez): rules that numbers and operations follow

sum (suhm): the answer to an addition problem

Index

Websites to Visit

www.aaamath.com/pro74b-propertiesmult.html

www.quia.com/ba/108397.html

www.quizlet.com/763838/scatter

About the Author

Lisa Arias is a math teacher who lives in Tampa, Florida with her husband and two children. Her out-of-the-box thinking and love for math guided her toward becoming an author. She enjoys playing board games and spending time with family and friends.

Meet The Author!
www.meetREMauthors.com

www.rourkeeducationalmedia.com

PHOTO CREDITS: Cover: © Phase Digital, Ljupco Smokovski; Page 4: © Ljupco Smokovski; Page 5: © Balehaa; Page 6:© Scottchan, Ljupco Smokovski, mschenk; Page 7: © Scruggelgreen; Page 24: © diane39; Page 27: © Ljupco

Edited by: Jill Sherman

Cover and Interior design by: Tara Raymo

Library of Congress PCN Data

Magical Mathematical Properties: Commutative, Associative, and Distributive / Lisa Arias
(Got Math!)
ISBN 978-1-62717-705-4 (hard cover)
ISBN 978-1-62717-827-3 (soft cover)
ISBN 978-1-62717-940-9 (e-Book)
Library of Congress Control Number: 2014935581

Printed in the United States of America, North Mankato, Minnesota

Also Available as: